HODDER SCIENCE

Pupil's Book
Second Edition

A

Nigel Heslop
David Brodie
James Williams

Hodder Murray
A MEMBER OF THE HODDER HEADLINE GROUP

The Publishers would like to thank the following for permission to reproduce copyright material:

BBC (bulldog report, 94); The webeducators (fertility timeline, 54)

Photo Acknowledgements
Action Plus (23 bottom, 69, 71 top, 74, 75, 76, 108 top)/ Jeff Morgan (87)/ Lyndon Beddoe (80 bottom middle)/ Melanie Friend, Photofusion Picture Library (80 centre)/ World through the lens (80 middle right); All Action (83); Alton Towers, Oblivion (80 top left) The Flume (80 bottom left); Andrew Lambert (21 bottom right, 63, 70 bottom, 98, 103 107 all, 109); Associated Press (139 bottom); BBC Natural History Unit (78, 126 bottom left)/ BBC Tomorrow's World (5 right); BBC Photo Library (94 right); Bob Battersby (13 right, 104 left); Bruce Coleman Limited (33 top, 71 bottom, 79, 121, 126 top left, top and bottom right, 127 bottom four photos); Corbis (2 right, 7 bottom, 13 left, 33 middle, 36 top, 94 left, 110, 128 top middle, 139 middle)/ Douglas P. Wilson, Frank Lane Picture Agency (128 bottom right)/ Frank W. Lane, Frank Lane/ Picture Agency (43 middle)/ Hal Beral (128 bottom middle)/ Jeffrey L. Rotman (128 top right) Michael S.. Lewis (80 bottom right)/ NASA (117)/ Ralph White (128 bottom left)/ Robert Landau (80 top middle)/ Roger Ressmeyer, NASA (128 top); David & Helen Litt (85 top); Getty Images/AFP (95); Galaxy Picture Library (147 second down on left and top right); Hodder & Stoughton (33 top left, 73, 88 right, 145 top); Holt Studios (85 bottom (both), 89 both, 127 top left); Home Office (139 top); Hugh S. Hudson (39); Hulton Getty (23 top); James Mayer (84); Leonard Hayflick (7 top); Life File (22 bottom (both), 32 middle right, 66 top, 97, 108 bottom, 134 top and bottom, 136); NASA (118 right); Natural History Museum (33 bottom); Nigel Heslop (20 right, 25, 102, 134 middle, 137); Oxford Scientific Films (5 left, 88 left, 122); Photodisc (141); Press Association (58, 92); REX/ John Gay (20 top left)/ Michael Huges (70 top); Ronald Grant Archive (28, 145 bottom); Science Museum/ Science & Society Picture Library (2 left and middle); Science Photo Library (147 top left)/ Alex Bartel (32 middle left and top right, 62)/ Andrew Syred (4 right and bottom left)/ Bernhard Edmaier (21 top right)/ Biophoto Associates (108 bottom)/ BSIP, Beranger (12 right)/ BSIP, Chagnon (108 top)/ CNRI (4 top left)/ Corey Meitchik, Custom Medical Stock Photo (48 second from bottom)/ Dan Schechter (143)/ David Nunuk (32 bottom right)/ Don Fawcett (47)/ Dr G Moscoso (48 third from top)/ Dr Ken Macdonald (top left)/ Dr Yorgos Nikas (48 left and top right)/ George Bernard (86)/ James Stevenson (48 bottom right)/ JC Revy (127 top right)/ John Heseltine (120 top)/ Mark Burnett (20 bottom left)/ Martin Dohrn (32 bottom left)/ Martyn F Chillmaid (114)/ NASA (118 bottom left, 119 top, 144 bottom, 147 bottom two on left)/ Novosti (144 top)/ Peter Chadwick (43 left)/ Peter Menzel (21 left)/ Petit Format, Nestle (48 second from top)/ Secchi-Lecaque, Roussel-UCLAF, CNRI (4 top right)/ Simon Fraser (12 left, 36, 120 middle and bottom)/ Stevie Grand (106)/ US Geological Survey (118 top left, 119 bottom); Still Pictures/ Carl R Sams II (43 right)/ Sue Cunningham (66 bottom); V & A Karl Witzmann/Johann Loetz Witwe Glassworks 1913 (104 top); Wellcome Trust, Medical Photographic Library (22 top left, 67)

Every effort has been made to trace all copyright holders, but if any have been inadvertently overlooked the Publishers will be pleased to make the necessary arrangements at the first opportunity.

Although every effort has been made to ensure that website addresses are correct at time of going to press, Hodder Murray cannot be held responsible for the content of any website mentioned in this book. It is sometimes possible to find a relocated web page by typing in the address of the home page for a website in the URL window of your browser.

Orders: please contact Bookpoint Ltd, 130 Milton Park, Abingdon, Oxon OX14 4SB. Telephone: (44) 01235 827720. Fax: (44) 01235 400454. Lines are open from 9.00–5.00, Monday to Saturday, with a 24-hour message answering service. Visit our website at www.hoddereducation.co.uk.

© 2000, 2004 Nigel Heslop, David Brodie, James Williams
First published 2000
This edition published 2004 by Hodder Murray, an imprint of the Hodder Education, a member of the Hodder Headline Group, an Hachette Livre UK Company
338 Euston Road London NW1 3BH

Impression number   10 9 8 7 6 5 4 3
Year   2010 2009 2008 2007

Cover photo Science Photo Library
Typeset in Garamond 11½/13 by Fakenham Photosetting, Norfolk
Printed in Italy

A catalogue record for this title is available from the British Library

ISBN: 978 0340 88671 7

Contents

Dedications

To my family, especially Will, for their inspiration and their perspiration.

Nigel Heslop

To my wife Joan, for her patience, understanding and practical advice, and to Laura and Sarah Grant for their expert advice in choosing the photographs.

James Williams

To Tom, Eleanor and Claire, not so much for being supportive as for being.

David Brodie

Picture this . . .

This section is to help you work out 'not understanding'.

Start off by reading this:

Everybody was there at junior school sports day. Luis, Maria, Vince and Serena had been friends since they all arrived in Britain with their parents, looking for a safe community to live in.

They lined up for the 60 metres sack race with two boys from another class. Maria had 'grown up' earlier than the others. She was much bigger and taller than her friends – her long legs seemed twice as long as theirs. She was bigger and stronger when they played games and they knew she would win for sure.

Miss Jack was the starter official. She was new to the school this year. They thought she looked cool with her bleached, braided hair and white Nike tracksuit. They concentrated on listening to her instruction.

The whistle blew and they were off. Some scuttled along and some hopped. The scuttlers put their feet in the corners of the sacks and ran. The hoppers pulled the sack up tight to their waist and hopped. Maria was a hopper, and a good one. By half-way she was well in front of the others, but then there was a crack and Maria fell to the ground with a scream.

The others were past her in no time and heard her whimper. At that moment the three friends turned, like synchronised swimmers, forgot the race and went back to comfort their friend.

Did you see the pictures in your head?

- School sports day
- Maria bigger and stronger than the others
- Miss Jack, the cool young teacher

And did the race play like a video in your head?

When you SEE THE PICTURES IN YOUR HEAD it means you understand what you are reading.

When you read or have something explained in science, try to make the pictures of what is happening appear in your head.

At first, perhaps it's just still pictures, of each stage in a description. You might see still pictures of Maria, the race, and Miss Jack. Then, if you concentrate hard, you can 'animate' the picture to make them play like a video. This is what UNDERSTANDING is like.

Task

Draw six boxes like this on your page. Look at each box in turn and imagine still pictures of the stages of making a cup of coffee for mum.

For example:

Coffee jar, milk and sugar	Kettle boiling	Spoon of coffee and sugar into cup
Add boiling water from kettle	Add milk	Stir and give to mum

Now imagine these still pictures and animate them to make them play together like a video. Can you see the whole process?

Working with words

Words usually have one meaning, but a word can have more than one meaning. This makes life a little bit complicated. So how are words constructed and can we work out what words mean in science?

Words are constructed like this.

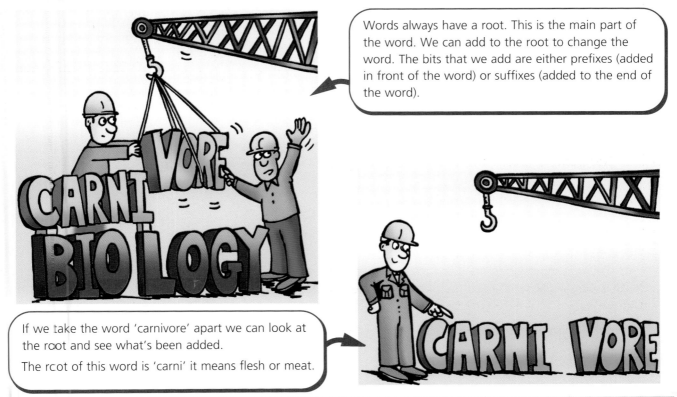

Words always have a root. This is the main part of the word. We can add to the root to change the word. The bits that we add are either prefixes (added in front of the word) or suffixes (added to the end of the word).

If we take the word 'carnivore' apart we can look at the root and see what's been added.

The root of this word is 'carni' it means flesh or meat.

The suffix '-vore' means feeding.

When we add the two togother we get the word 'carnivore' which means meat eater or meat feeder. The word Bronchitis is made up in the same way. The root of the word is 'bronch' meaning windpipe and the suffix 'itis' simply means inflammed or diseased. So 'bronchitis' means that your windpipe is inflamed – something that gives you a cough!

Task

See how many meanings, of the words below, you can work out from the table of roots, prefixes and suffixes shown.

- Biology
- Herbicide
- tetrapod

- carnivore
- endodermis

Root	Meaning
dermis	skin
bio	life
pod(o)	leg/foot
herbi	plant
carni	meat/flesh

Prefix	Meaning
endo	inside
tetra	four

Suffix	Meaning
logy	study
cide	killing
vore	feeding

Life

Opener Activity
What are living organisms made from?

Yes, Argooo, I've investigated the new life form; this is it!

So Krach, you've compared it with our definition of life?

Yes, it excretes, needs food, senses things around it, moves, needs oxygen to burn fuel for energy, and it must reproduce as there are so many little ones running around. And some have extra bits and fins which must have grown.

Ok, then we must locate the leader and make friends with this life form!

Activity

Modern cars are 'intelligent'. They can talk to us, tell us when they need fuel, when they need a service. In fact, they can do almost everything that a living organism can do. So why is a car not a living thing?

Krach and Argooo think that cars are living things. Think back to work you have done on living things. Do you remember MRS GREN?

1 Explain what a car does or has that makes it similar to a living thing. Put your answers into a table.

2 Now write and tell Krach and Argooo why a car is not a living thing.

Characteristic	Car	Human
M ovement		
R espiration		
S ensitivity		
G rowth		
R eproduction		
E xcretion		
N utrition		

Cells

All living organisms are made up of cells.

Robert Hooke

In 1665 a scientist called Robert Hooke published a book called *Micrographia*. His book was all about what you could see under a microscope. In this book he used the word **cell** for the first time. He was describing what cork looked like, and thought that the box shapes he could see were like the rooms that monks lived in, called cells. Today the word cell describes what all living things are made up of. Unlike Robert Hooke's empty boxes, we know that cells are not empty but full of important structures and chemicals.

Figure 2 Robert Hooke using his simple microscope

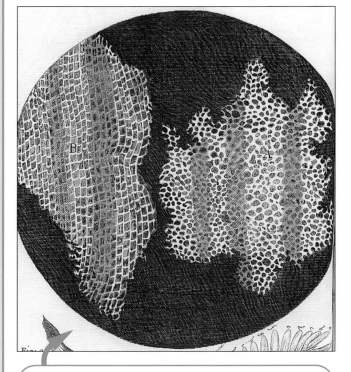

Figure 1 Hooke's drawing of the cells in cork

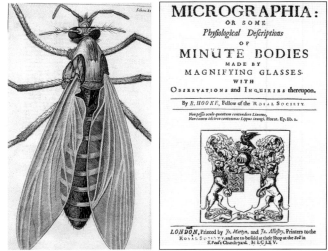

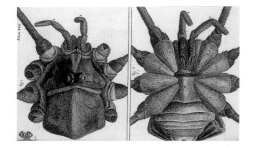

Figure 3 Some drawings from Hooke's book *Micrographia*

Cell structure

Plant and animal cells have a number of things in common and a few differences.

Figure 2 shows you what a typical animal cell and a typical plant cell look like.

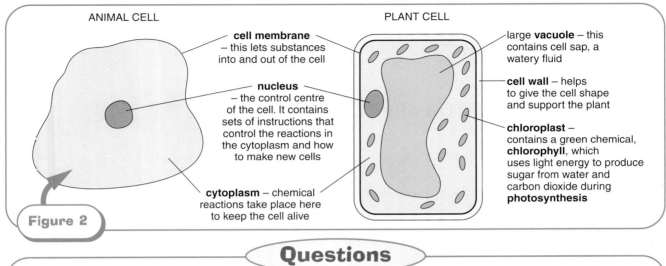

ANIMAL CELL

cell membrane – this lets substances into and out of the cell

nucleus – the control centre of the cell. It contains sets of instructions that control the reactions in the cytoplasm and how to make new cells

cytoplasm – chemical reactions take place here to keep the cell alive

Figure 2

PLANT CELL

large **vacuole** – this contains cell sap, a watery fluid

cell wall – helps to give the cell shape and support the plant

chloroplast – contains a green chemical, **chlorophyll**, which uses light energy to produce sugar from water and carbon dioxide during **photosynthesis**

Questions

1 Copy out the following table under the heading 'Cells'. Put a tick if a structure is present in the cell and a cross if it is not. Use the diagrams to help you.

Cell structure	Animal cell	Plant cell
cell membrane	✓	✓
cell wall		
cytoplasm		
nucleus		
large vacuole		
chloroplast		

2 Plants have a cell wall that helps to give the cell shape. What do humans have to give them support and shape?

3 Chloroplasts in plant cells use water and carbon dioxide to make sugar. They join these two chemicals together using the energy from sunlight. This process is known as **photosynthesis**. Where could the plant get the following:

a) carbon dioxide?

b) water?

4 As a plant loses water, the large vacuole inside its cells gets smaller, but the cells do not lose their shape because of the strong cell walls. This means that the plant does not collapse. When the cell gets more water again, the large vacuole increases in size. Draw a strip cartoon to show what happens. Write a story under each picture to explain what is happening.

Remember

Fill in the blanks in the passage below.

cell wall   nucleus   cells   vacuole   cell membrane   nucleus   cytoplasm

All living things are made up of _____1_____. Plant and animal cells have a _____2_____ _____, _____3_____ and _____4_____. Plant cells also have a _____5_____ _____, and a _____6_____. Cells are controlled by the _____7_____. Chemical reactions, which keep the cell alive, take place in the cytoplasm.

Tissues

Groups of cells of the same kind are called a tissue. Tissues carry out different jobs or **functions**.

Different cells, different functions!

Different cells have different functions. Some make things, others control things. Some protect us, others provide support. They often work together in groups.

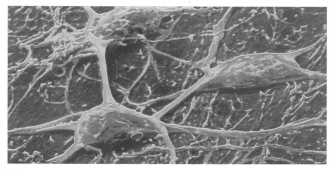

a) Sperm cells

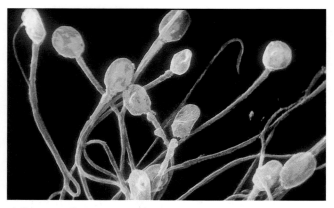

b) Nerve cells

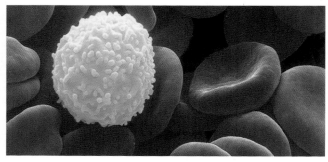

c) Red and white blood cells

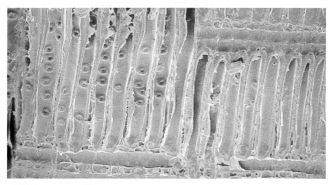

d) Xylem vessels

Figure 1 Plant and animal cells come in different shapes and sizes

Animal tissue	Function
skin	to protect the body and stop harmful things entering
blood	to carry oxygen, carbon dioxide and chemicals from food around the body
bone	to give support
nervous tissue	to carry messages
muscle	to help us move

Plant tissue	Function
xylem	to carry water and minerals from the roots to the leaves
phloem	to carry food dissolved in water around the plant

Table 1 Some examples of animal and plant tissues

Growing tissues

Some animals and plants can replace damaged parts and tissues. Humans do this when we repair cuts and broken bones. Large parts of plants can be cut off without the plant dying. Gardeners deliberately prune some plants to make them grow.

A starfish can replace one of its 'arms' if it is eaten by a larger animal. Regrowing damaged parts is called **regeneration**. Some people think that if you cut a worm in two you will have two worms. This is not true. The top half may grow a new tail but the tail end will die.

surgeons to repair tissue that has been badly damaged and help rebuild a person's ear.

Figure 2 The starfish will regenerate a missing 'arm'. A person cannot do this, but we can regenerate a fingernail that gets lost in an accident.

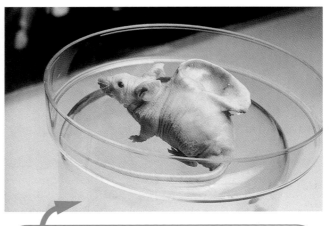

Figure 3 Scientists covered a mesh in the shape of a human ear with mouse cells. As these cells grew, the mesh dissolved leaving mouse tissue. This ear was transplanted onto the mouse.

Plant and animal tissues can be grown outside the body. Scientists do this for a number of reasons, for example to study cells better, or to replace damaged tissue. When tissues are grown like this they are called **tissue cultures**. They have to be grown in very clean or **sterile** conditions. In order for the cells to grow they need nutrients or food. A special jelly called a **culture medium** provides this. If you take the tip off the shoot of a plant and grow this in a culture medium, you can grow a whole new set of shoots, leaves and flowers. When this is planted in soil, the plant will develop roots.

Scientists can grow human skin to replace skin that has been damaged in a fire. Recently, scientists have been looking at ways of making new tissue grow over a shape. This could enable

Questions

1 What do we mean by a 'tissue culture'?

2 Small cuts heal leaving no marks. If you get a deep cut, what can happen when it heals?

3 Why do tissue cultures need sterile conditions?

4 Scientists might be able to grow the shape of an ear. What could be stopping them growing a finger or hand?

Remember

Unscramble the words on each line to make a sentence. Copy the sentences into your exercise book.

a) cells   different   different   jobs   have

b) same kind   called a tissue   group of cells   of the   are

c) called tissue cultures   can be grown plant and animal tissues   outside the body   these are

New cells from old

Cells in our bodies are continually being replaced.

Growth

You are not the same person today as when you were born. It may sound silly, but it's true. Since you were born you have grown and developed. In fact you no longer have any of the cells in your body that you were born with! As we grow and develop, the cells, tissues and organs in our body grow and change. How do they do this? Well, cells are always being replaced and old cells die and get broken down in our bodies. In fact in the time it has taken to read this paragraph, many of the cells in your body have died and many new ones have taken their place. A normal cell does not live forever.

All of the cells in our body, except mature red blood cells, have a **nucleus**. The nucleus controls what the cell does (its function) and when and how it should divide. Look at the cartoon strip opposite to see how cells divide. Cells make copies of themselves when they divide.

In 1961, a cancer scientist called Leonard Hayflick found out that normal human cells eventually die. He also noticed that the oldest cells he grew in his lab usually died first. Hayflick suspected that cells contain some sort of clock that tells them when it is time to stop dividing. Later he discovered that cells have what he called an 'event counter' – this counts the number of times a group of cells will double, *not* how long the cell has been alive. Most groups of cells can double between 50 and 100 times before they die completely. Some cells, such as red and white blood cells, can double many more times. Other cells, like nerve cells, cannot double at all. A small group of two cells that doubles three times would end up as a group of 16 cells. Two cells double to four, four cells double to eight, and eight cells double to 16.

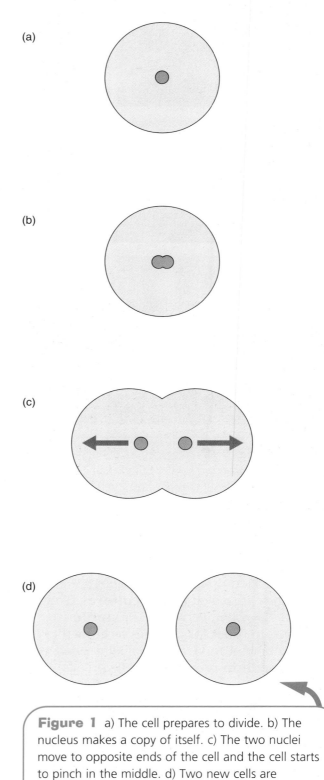

(a)

(b)

(c)

(d)

Figure 1 a) The cell prepares to divide. b) The nucleus makes a copy of itself. c) The two nuclei move to opposite ends of the cell and the cell starts to pinch in the middle. d) Two new cells are produced identical to the first cell.

Figure 2 Leonard Hayflick

Figure 3 The late actor Christopher Reeve was paralysed in a horse riding accident. He damaged his nervous system and since his nerve cells were unable to repair themselves, he was not able to walk afterwards.

Questions

1 Which cells are the only cells not to have a nucleus when they are mature?

2 Red blood cells do not divide as they travel around our blood vessels. Why can't they divide here and what could happen if they did divide as they travelled in our bloodstream?

3 Cells are often given what scientists call a 'Hayflick limit', that is the number of times the cells will be able to double before they die. If a group of cells had a Hayflick limit of 5, how many new cells could one of these cells produce before the cells die? (Show how you worked this out. You might also want to make a line graph to show how many cells there are after the first, second, third doubling and so on.)

4 If you damage nerve cells they will often not repair themselves. Nerve cells cannot divide to make new nerve cells. Imagine that someone badly cuts their hand and cuts through nerve cells leading to the fingers, what might happen and what effect might this have on them?

Remember

Use the words given here to complete the sentences below.

**die   live   copies   blood   nucleus
divide   decides**

Cells do not ____1____ forever. They make ____2____ of themselves and die.

All cells have a nucleus except red ____3____ cells. The ____4____ controls the cell and ____5____ when it should ____6____ and when it should ____7____.

Henrietta Lacks and her immortal cells

Cancer cells can divide forever and never die.

Henrietta Lacks was born in 1920 in a town called Clover in the United States of America. Although she died of cancer in 1953, some of the cells from her body that she donated to science are still alive and reproducing. The cells have no Hayflick limit. They have helped scientists to learn about cancer and also help doctors in their research into diseases such as polio. Henrietta's cells have made her immortal and many people's lives have been saved because of what scientists have found out through studying them.

Henrietta Lacks lived a happy normal life with her husband David, moving to the town of Turner's Station near Baltimore. She had five children and then, after the birth of her fifth child in 1951, she became ill. She was admitted to Johns Hopkins University Hospital and was found to be suffering from a type of cancer that only affects women – cancer of the cervix (the cervix is found at the entrance to the womb). This resulted in an uncontrolled growth of tissue called a **tumour**. In the 1950s, treatment for cancer was not very advanced and many women died. Today, about 4500 cases of cancer of the cervix are diagnosed in this country every year, but if found and treated in its early stages, it can be successfully cured.

Henrietta let Dr George Gey take a sample of the cancer cells from the tumour she had developed. Dr Gey was working on ways of growing human cells outside the body. Normal cells he had tried to grow did not survive long once they had been removed from the body. The cells he had from Henrietta Lacks, however, kept on growing and dividing and did not die like samples from other people. In order to keep Henrietta's identity secret and to avoid upsetting her family, he called the cells HeLa cells. HeLa cells are still being reproduced today, nearly 50 years after her death and scientists all over the world use them in their research into cancer.

Looking for cancer

Tumours can be either **benign** or **malignant**. Benign tumours are not cancer. They can usually be removed without any problem. It is the malignant tumours which are cancer.

Cancer can often be found before the disease causes symptoms. Checking for cancer (or for conditions that may lead to cancer) in a person who does not have any symptoms of the disease is called **screening**.

Screening may involve a physical examination, medical tests or scans. During a physical exam, the doctor looks for anything unusual and feels for any lumps or growths. Examples of laboratory tests include blood and urine tests and looking through a microscope at cells. Scans involve the use of X-ray images (such as mammograms to check the breasts).

In a special kind of X-ray imaging, a CT or CAT scan uses a computer linked to an X-ray machine to make a series of detailed pictures of the inside of the body.

What is cancer?

Cancer is the uncontrolled division of cells. A cancerous cell will keep on dividing and each of the cells it produces also keeps on dividing. Eventually a tumour can form. Cancerous cells can also travel around the body in the bloodstream and new tumours can be produced at other sites in the body. Many things can cause cancer, including exposure to radioactivity, strong chemicals and too much sunbathing.

Not all cancers will kill you. Many cancers can be treated if caught early, by **radiotherapy** (killing the cancer cells with radiation), **chemotherapy** (killing the cells with powerful drugs) or removing the cancerous cells by **surgery** (cutting them out of the body). The likelihood of someone getting cancer will vary with age.

You are very unlikely to have cancer as a child or young person. The older you are, the greater the chance of having some type of cancer. It is not just found in humans though – cats, dogs, farm animals, birds and fish can all suffer from cancer.

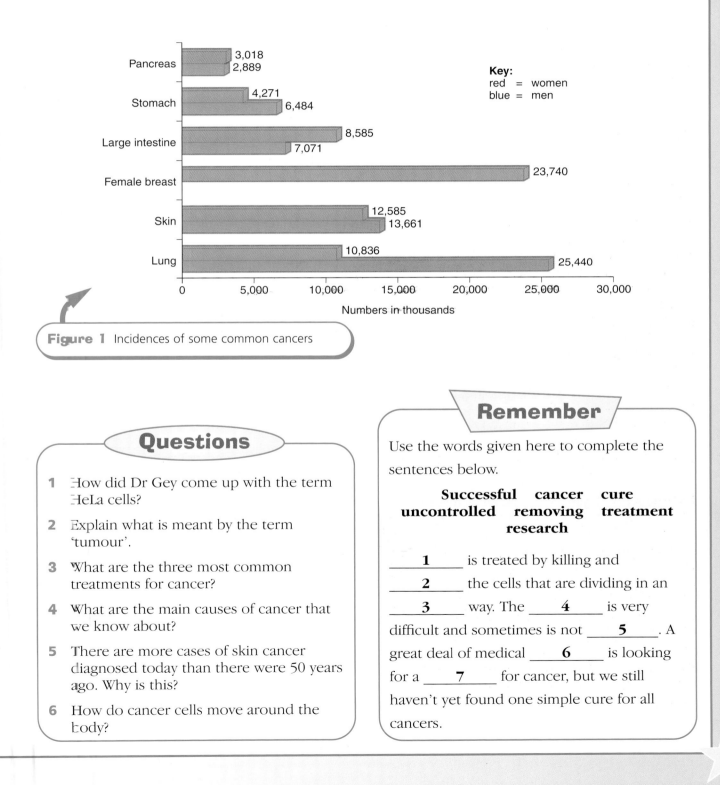

Figure 1 Incidences of some common cancers

Questions

1 How did Dr Gey come up with the term HeLa cells?

2 Explain what is meant by the term 'tumour'.

3 What are the three most common treatments for cancer?

4 What are the main causes of cancer that we know about?

5 There are more cases of skin cancer diagnosed today than there were 50 years ago. Why is this?

6 How do cancer cells move around the body?

Remember

Use the words given here to complete the sentences below.

**Successful   cancer   cure
uncontrolled   removing   treatment
research**

_____1_____ is treated by killing and _____2_____ the cells that are dividing in an _____3_____ way. The _____4_____ is very difficult and sometimes is not _____5_____. A great deal of medical _____6_____ is looking for a _____7_____ for cancer, but we still haven't yet found one simple cure for all cancers.

Are you irreplaceable?

Although the cells in our bodies are continually dividing, we cannot re-grow limbs or organs, unlike the starfish on page 5. If our organs become damaged, we may need an **organ transplant**.

You may be surprised to learn that you can live without quite a lot of your body. Even so, it is still best to hang on to what you have for as long as you can and look after it carefully.

Body part	How can you live without it?
skull cap	Your skull protects your brain but metal plates can be used instead.
arms/legs	Many people have lost an arm or a leg in an accident. You can adapt to living without a limb or you can have a replacement false limb fitted.
liver	You can lose $\frac{3}{4}$ of your liver without serious problems. In children the liver can grow back!
spleen	The spleen breaks down old red blood cells. You can live without one.
appendix	This section of your intestine can be removed with no problems.
gall bladder	This produces bile that neutralises the acid which is added to your food in the stomach. You have to be careful what you eat but you can live without it.
pancreas	This makes enzymes that break down food. If this is removed, you have to take medication for the rest of your life.
stomach	Most of your stomach can go. It adds acid to your food but most digestion takes place in the small intestine.
large intestine	This takes water from the food passing through your body. You do not need it all to live.
small intestine	Most of the digestion of your food happens here. The small intestine is several feet long and you could lose most of it, although you might have to be fed through a tube with a mixture that is partly digested. Not very tasty!
kidney	You have two kidneys and you can happily lead a normal life with just one. Damage that and you may need a replacement or some artificial help.
reproductive organs	None of these are essential to life and can be removed if they have cancer. They produce chemicals called hormones which have to be replaced.
thyroid gland	This produces chemicals that control your growth. If you have this taken away you will need medication for life.
adrenal gland	This produces hormones. Without it you will need to take hormone replacements for ever.

Table 1

Groups of cells form tissues and groups of tissues form organs. Organs make up organ systems and organ systems working together add up to a living organism.

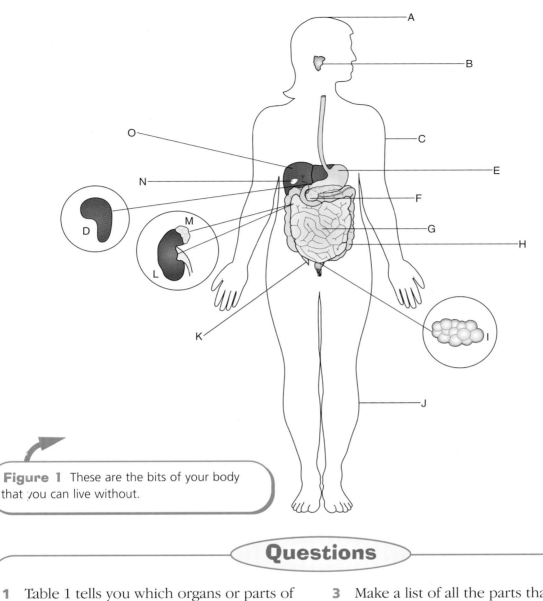

Figure 1 These are the bits of your body that you can live without.

Questions

1 Table 1 tells you which organs or parts of the body you could lose and still live a near normal life. Make a list of the parts and match them to the letters on the diagram.

2 **a)** Name three essential parts of your body that you cannot lose and stay alive.

   b) Explain why you cannot live without each of these.

3 Make a list of all the parts that can be lost and cause a person no bother at all.

4 Copy and fill in the table opposite using the information from Table 1.

Medical help needed if this body part is lost	Type of medical help needed

Remember

Unscramble these names for body parts you can do without.

NIYKED   LENEPS   HAMCOTS   XIPADPEN   GELS   RODHITY   VILER

Closer

Who's who in diagnosing and treating cancer

Cancer is a serious medical condition, but many cancers can be treated and cured if diagnosed early enough. The diagnosis and treatment of cancer normally begins with your own doctor or GP.

Your GP

If you have any strange lumps on your body, you should see your doctor (General Practitioner – GP). Your GP will examine you and arrange any further tests. You may be referred to a specialist clinic or hospital.

At the clinic

A specialist doctor will take your medical history and give you a physical examination. You may have an X-ray and blood test.

After diagnosis

If the tests confirm that someone has cancer, the treatment can vary.

Surgery

A surgeon will operate and remove the cancerous cells to prevent them growing and spreading around the body. Sometimes the cancerous parts are frozen and then cut out. This is known as **cryosurgery** (the prefix *cryo* means frost or ice).

Chemotherapy

Chemotherapy is the treatment of cancer with drugs that destroy cancer cells. They are called 'anticancer' drugs. They destroy cancer cells by stopping them from growing or multiplying. Some healthy cells can also be killed, this is what causes side effects, like hair falling out. Normal cells usually repair themselves.

Radiotherapy

X-rays, gamma-rays, and other types of radioactivity are used to kill cancer cells and shrink tumours. The radiation can come from a machine outside the body, or it may come from radioactive material placed in the body near cancer cells.

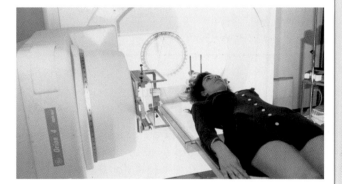

Activity

1 Find out about the different types of doctors you can find at a hospital and what they treat. You could use a dictionary or search the internet.

2 What do the following doctors specialise in?

   a) mycologist **b)** epidemiologist **c)** dermatologist **d)** psychologist

   e) audiologist **f)** cytologist **g)** ophthalmologist **h)** haematologist

Opener Activity
What is the matter?

Matter is a scientific word for all the 'stuff' that everything is made from.

Matter comes in bits. But what happens if you keep cutting up matter? Can you go on cutting it into smaller and smaller bits forever? Do you get tiny bits (particles) that are so small they can't be cut up any more?

Ideas like this puzzle scientists. They need to be able to explain what matter is like. Here are some clues.

A tiny amount of oil spilt onto water will spread out into a very thin layer.

Lots of air can be squashed into one small tyre to make it hard but bouncy.

You can make the orange very, very dilute and still taste it.

The scientists formed a **theory** to explain how things worked. They did this by collecting lots of **observations** about natural things, like those in the photos. Then they used their **imagination** to put these ideas together. They were helped by previous ideas but they improved on them.

They used their new **theory** to make predictions. They tested the theory with **experiments**.

The more **reliable** their predictions were in giving the right answer, the more **confidence** they had in their theory.

The theory which scientists now have is that all matter is made of tiny individual particles that can't be cut up. They are really tiny. There are about 10 million particles to a millimetre.

Questions

Use the particles theory above to explain these observations in the questions below.

1 A sponge can absorb water from a dripping tap without it running out from the bottom.

2 If you pour a glass of lemonade the bubbles continue to appear from the bottom of the glass.

3 Some balloons that you buy float up in the air, those that you blow up yourself don't.

4 You breathe in the same amount as you breathe out, but the air has changed. How does this happen?

5 You roll up a sleeping bag to pack it, but once it reaches a certain size it won't go any smaller.

Carnival people

All matter is made of tiny particles. They move about constantly, even in solids. This is called the **Kinetic Theory of Matter**.

A wild time

Figure 1 Carnival at the Sambadrome

Thinking about particles

Solid, liquid and gas are called the three **states of matter**. They are all very different because of the way the particles move about and how the particles are packed together.

The particles are tiny. Smaller than anything you could imagine – far too small to see. But all these particles are moving all the time.

They behave rather like the people at a crowded carnival.

Solid in the stand

The particles in a **solid** are like the people sitting in the stands at a carnival. Each person has a fixed place and the people next to them do not change. The people have no spaces between them. They are all in neat rows.

Because they are packed neatly together they are in a shape that has straight edges. The people can move about a little, backwards and forwards, to and fro, but they do not move out of their place in the crowd. The block of people always stays the same shape, even though the people are moving.

Liquid crowds

The people standing in the crowd at the carnival are like the particles in a **liquid**. They are all pushed together so that there are no spaces between them. But they are in a jumble and do not have fixed positions. The people can move past each other. With the movements in the crowd, people can change position quite a lot. They can have different people next to them. They can move past each other to get a different place. Just like particles in a liquid they will take the shape of the 'container'. It could be a long, thin pavement or a square section of space. At the carnival it's the barriers that hold the crowd in its shape.

The performers are a gas

Gas particles are like the people dancing. They are all moving about very quickly and often bump into each other.

Gases need to be kept in a container. This is because the particles move about all the time. The container is like the barriers at the sides of the procession.

Gases mix easily with each other, that is how a smell spreads through air – the smell is carried by a gas. This is called **diffusion**.

Questions

1 Draw a picture of the people in the stands. The seats are so close together that their shoulders touch and their knees are against the shoulders of the people below them.

2 Imagine you are in the stands at the Sambadrome. Explain how you could move a little without leaving your seat.

3 Draw a picture of the people in the crowd as a random jumble of faces.

4 Write about when you have been in crowds that are packed tightly together. Explain how you were able to move.

5 A gas would be like people running round in the school hall. Draw a picture of this.

6 What would make the people in your picture from Question 5 *have* to change direction?

7 What would be the difference to your picture from Question 5 if the people were running round on the school field?

Remember

Copy these sentences and draw pictures to show what they mean.

- Particles in a **solid** are touching each other. They have fixed positions but **vibrate**.
- Particles in a **liquid** are pushed together and touch, but move about **randomly**.
- Particles in a **gas** are **separate** from each other. They move about very **quickly**.
- Scientists call this the **Kinetic Theory**. Kinetic means movement.

2.2

A closer look at carnival people

The arrangement of particles can explain the properties of solids, liquids and gases.

Making a thinking model

Figure 1 Watching the carnival from the stands

On the previous page you imagined particles of matter as people. This is the 'model' you are using to help you make a picture happen in your head.

All the particles in solids, liquids and gases have some energy. The particles are moving all the time, even in solids. This idea of particles moving is called the **Kinetic Theory of Matter**.

This 'model' can be used to explain things – like what is happening when a solid heats up.

If you make the people more excited – like when there is louder music – then they move about more. This is like making a solid more 'excited' by giving it extra energy. This makes its temperature higher and its particles vibrate faster.

Figure 2 Standing in the crowd at the carnival

Questions

Match the properties of matter for solids to sentences in Questions 1 to 4. Explain how the properties are 'modelled' by the carnival crowd seated in the stands.

Properties

   i) Solids don't mix

   ii) Solids can't be compressed

   iii) Solids have a fixed shape

   iv) Solids have a fixed volume

1 Every person has a fixed place. They are all in neat rows, in a shape that has straight edges.

2 There are no spaces between them and they could not be pushed closer together.

3 The block of people stays the same size, even though the people are moving to and fro.

4 The people next to them do not change position so they don't get mixed up.

Questions

Match the properties of matter for liquids to sentences in Questions 5 to 7. Explain how these are 'modelled' by the people standing in the carnival crowd.

Properties

   i) Liquids have no fixed shape

   ii) Liquids can't be compressed

   iii) Liquids can mix (diffuse) together

5 The people are all pushed together. There are no spaces between them.

6 The people are in a jumble and do not have fixed positions.

7 They can move past each other to get a different place with different people next to them.

Match the properties of matter for a gas to sentences in Questions 8 and 9. Explain how these are 'modelled' by the carnival dancers.

Properties

   i) Gases exert a pressure on the walls of their container

   ii) Gases have no fixed volume

8 They are moving about very quickly and often bumping into the barriers at the sides.

9 The barriers at the sides are needed to keep the people in place.

The dancers

There are big gaps between the performers. Two parts of the carnival can mix together. The carnival procession could go through a narrower space if it needed to. This is like squashing a gas. Gases are easy to compress and they diffuse and mix.

Figure 3 Dancers at the carnival

Remember

Use the words given here to complete the sentences below.

| **Volume** | **fixed** | **shape** | **compressed** | **compress** | **diffuse** | **pressure** |

Particle ideas can explain that solids have a ____**1**____ shape and a fixed ____**2**____. Solids don't diffuse into each other.

Liquids have no fixed ____**3**____ but do have a fixed volume. Liquids can't be ____**4**____.

Gases are easy to ____**5**____. They exert a ____**6**____ on their container. They ____**7**____ into each other.

Hard lessons

Hardness can be explained by thinking about how strongly the particles hold on to one another in a solid.

Think about the materials you have cut up to make models in school. Some materials are easy to cut and some are hard.

Wood and plastic are easier to cut than metal. This is because the forces between particles are stronger in metals than in wood and plastic. Some wood can be pulled apart into fibres. The forces holding the wood particles together in a fibre are stronger than those holding one fibre to another.

Soft materials like wax, plasticine and clay have particles that hold on to each other very weakly. They can be easily squashed into a new shape. But if you bake clay models in a kiln, you get a change which makes very strong forces between the particles. These new ceramic materials are very hard to cut. The strong forces make ceramic materials very inflexible and they break apart if you try to bend them.

> **Figure 1** This is what would happen if you tried to saw metal with a wooden saw.

Questions

1 A saw to cut wood is made of metal. Explain how you can tell that wood particles are held together less strongly than particles in metals?

2 There is a scale of hardness. The lowest material on the scale is a soft material called talc. The hardest material known is diamond.

   Put these materials in order of hardness, starting with the hardest:

   **dry clay   steel drill   brick
   candle wax   stone   soap**

3 Draw particle cartoons to illustrate the different hardness of wax and stone.

4 People say 'the hardest material known is diamond.' How would you get *evidence* to prove this statement?

   Explain how you could gather evidence from a) experiments, b) other people, c) scientific sources such as textbooks and the Internet.

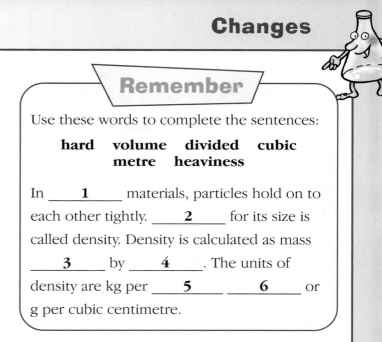

Density

A trick question often asked is 'which is heavier, a kilogram of feathers or a kilogram of stones'. The answer is they both have the same mass – one kilogram of course. But people are fooled in their thinking because stones are 'heavier for their size' than feathers.

Metals are most often heavier for their size than other materials. This is because the metal particles are heavier compared to the particles in wood and plastic.

The property 'heaviness for its size' has a proper name. It's called **density**. Look at Table 1 showing the density of some objects. Density is measured in the table in 'g/cm³'. This is how many grams each centimetre cube of the material weighs. Often density is measured as 'kg/m³', which is how many kilograms a metre cube of the material weighs. A metre cube is almost the size of four washing machines – a big lump of material indeed!

Remember

Use these words to complete the sentences:

**hard   volume   divided   cubic
metre   heaviness**

In _____1_____ materials, particles hold on to each other tightly. _____2_____ for its size is called density. Density is calculated as mass _____3_____ by _____4_____. The units of density are kg per _____5_____ _____6_____ or g per cubic centimetre.

This formula can be used to work out the density of an object.

$$\text{Density of material} = \frac{\text{Mass of object}}{\text{Volume of object}}$$

Questions

5 Use the formula above and a calculator to complete this table.

Object	Material	Mass/g	Volume/cm³	Density/g/cm³
wooden desk	wood	35000	70000	_____
key	steel	38.5	5	_____
chopping board	wood	1200	2400	_____
fishing weight	lead	22	2	_____
club hammer	steel	5800	750	_____
floor tile	marble	4000	_____	2.2
safety glasses	Perspex	_____	50	1.2

Table 1

6 When you are washing up, what are the things that feel heaviest for their size? Does this agree with the densities in the table?

7 If you threw a key and a wooden desk into a river, the desk would float. Why?

8 List the materials in the table in order of density. Use a computer to produce a bar chart (if there is one available).

Expansion

When most materials are heated they increase in size. For solids and liquids the increase is small but it carries a great deal of force. Gases expand much more.

Designer's headaches

Figure 1 This plane is breaking the sound barrier. After the sonic boom the air expands and cools rapidly. Water vapour condenses out as a cloud.

Figure 2 Expansion joint of a bridge

Motorway bridges are made of big solid slabs. When they are baking hot on a summer day they also increase in length. The problem is not the increase, but the enormous force that the expansion causes. This could buckle and crack the bridge. There have to be special sliding joints built in like the ones in Figure 2. These cope with the changing forces and the changing length of the bridge.

Thermometers

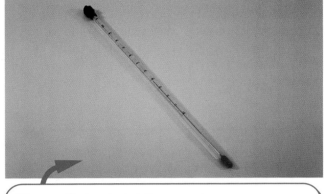

Figure 3 An alcohol thermometer

When the liquid in the thermometer in Figure 3 is heated it expands up the narrow tube above the bulb. Because the tube is narrow, a small change in temperature and a small expansion of the liquid makes a big difference to the level in the tube.

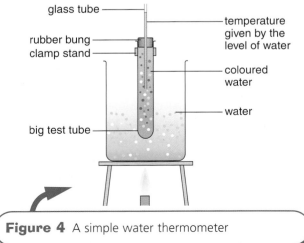

glass tube

rubber bung

clamp stand

big test tube

temperature given by the level of water

coloured water

water

Figure 4 A simple water thermometer

Questions

Look at the diagram of a simple thermometer in Figure 4.

1 When the beaker of water is heated, what will happen to the level of the water in the tube?

2 This thermometer would be no use to measure the temperature in a freezer. Write two sentences to explain why.

Up, up and away

Hot air balloons are simple things. They have a gas burner, a big bag to catch the hot air and a basket. When air is hot it expands a great deal. This makes it lighter for its size (i.e. less dense) than the normal air around it. Because it is less dense, it will float up in the normal air.

Figure 5 A gathering of hot air balloons.

Ice is the odd one out

Nearly all solids expand when they melt and contract when they solidify. But the ice/water change is different.

Ice cubes always float in a glass of water. They must therefore be less heavy for their size than the water around them. Water must expand when it freezes. If you look at an ice cube tray you can see that the level has risen up in each square of the tray.

Figure 6 Because water expands as it freezes . . . icebergs float on top of the sea.

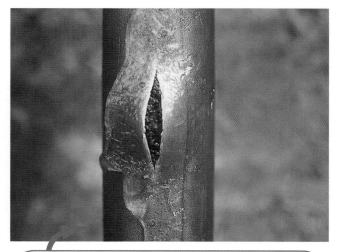

Figure 7 Because water expands as it freezes . . . the ice has swelled up inside this water pipe and made cracks in the metal.

Remember

Complete the sentences using the words below.

solids bigger same expand lot melt

Nearly all materials ____**1**____ on heating and contract when they cool. But their mass stays the ____**2**____ .

Gases expand a ____**3**____ more than ____**4**____ and liquids. Nearly all solids expand when they ____**5**____ . Ice is odd. Water gets ____**6**____ when it turns into ice.

Stretchy and bendy

Solid particles are in a rigid arrangement. Liquid particles are in a crowded jumble. Gas particles whiz about apart from each other.

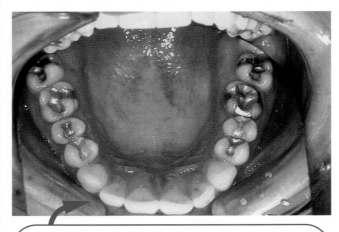

Figure 1 If the fillings were harder than the tooth enamel, they would damage the surrounding teeth. Dentists often use gold to replace teeth because it has the right hardness.

Figure 2 Wood is flexible. This is helped because the particles in wood are long and thin so they bend without breaking.

Figure 3 Rubber is stretchy. The particles in rubber are folded up like a zigzag. When the rubber is pulled, the zigzag particles straighten out without breaking.

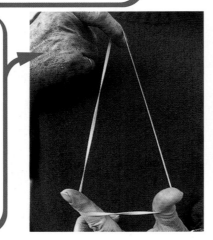

Questions

1 When clothes are repaired, the 'stretchiness' of the repair material has to be the same as that of the cloth. Explain why.

2 Draw pictures to show how particles are arranged in wood and rubber when they are unstretched and when they are bent or stretched.

Hitting the water

It hurts when you dive into a pool and do a 'belly flop'. But when you climb down the ladder, the liquid water is soft, not hard.

Particles in a liquid have the same arrangement as the balls in a children's ball pond.

The particles are close together but in a jumble. Step into the ball pond and you can sink right through it. Your legs feel no resistance as they push the particles apart.

The ball pond will take the shape of whatever room or space it is in. But if you 'belly flop' into the ball pond from high up, there is no time for the particles to push apart before they stop your fall. Ouch! That's why a belly flop into water hurts.

Figure 4 Children playing in a ball pond.

A soft landing

Before the invention of modern equipment, pole-vaulters had to practise their event by landing in soft sand. This has now been replaced by the modern 'crash mat'. It's full of air, and that absorbs the energy of the pole-vaulter, slowing them down to a soft landing. Sometimes the athletes even land head first!

Figure 5 A pole-vaulter from 1933 (top). A modern pole-vaulter (bottom).

Gases are the most squashable of all materials. The particles in air are separated from each

other. They whiz about very quickly and collide with the walls of the container they are in, pushing on it.

If a pole-vaulter lands on the crash mat, the air particles get pushed closer together making the soft landing. The air particles move about all the time. When the pole-vaulter climbs off the mat, they push it back into its original shape from the inside. This is a result of **air pressure**. An air bag in a car does a similar job.

Questions

3 Draw a strip cartoon showing a belly flop into a ball pond. Add speech bubbles to it. Explain what has happened using scientific words.

4 What would be the effect on the pole vaulter if the crash mat was filled with water instead of air? Would this be better or worse than landing on sand? Explain why.

5 Write a short newspaper article with illustrations to explain how safety air bags in cars work. Use these ideas:

- Compressed air is in a small gas bottle inside the steering wheel.
- A sensor detects a crash.
- The air bag inflates rapidly.
- It stops the driver's head hitting anything hard.

Remember

Copy this paragraph and learn the ideas.

Solid materials stay in one shape. They can be broken up or bent by a force, but they stay the same size.

Liquids go into the shape of the container into which they are poured, but their size (volume) stays the same.

Gases can be squashed into a smaller size and shape. They will also spread out to fill all of a space.

2.6 Always moving and mixing

Liquids and gases **flow**. They take up the shape of the bottle or jar they are in.

Liquids are soft. The particles are easily pushed apart.

Figure 1 The crowd at the carnival take the shape of the space behind the barrier.

Liquids fill up whatever shape of space there is. But the particles do not stand still. They move past each other freely even though they are packed close together.

Figure 2 The dancers spread out into the space available.

Gases flow, the particles are far apart and are moving about quickly. Gases spread to take up all the space in whatever container they are in. The gas particles move about everywhere, sometimes bumping into each other or bouncing back from the walls. The force of them bumping into the walls creates the gas pressure.

Brownian motion

Specks of smoke or dust in a gas or liquid can be seen to move about randomly. The movement of the specks is called **Brownian motion**. The gas particles are too small to reflect the light in a smoke cell, but they make the bigger smoke specks jiggle about as they hit them. You can see the movement of the smoke specks with a microscope.

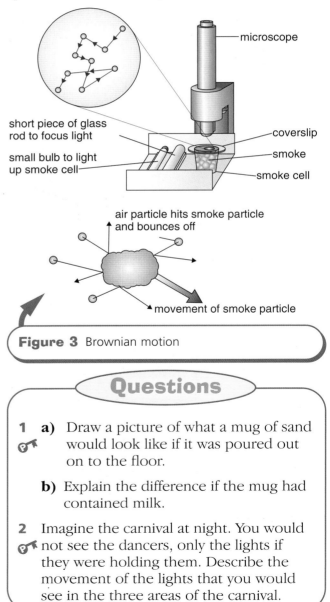

Figure 3 Brownian motion

Questions

1 a) Draw a picture of what a mug of sand would look like if it was poured out on to the floor.

   b) Explain the difference if the mug had contained milk.

2 Imagine the carnival at night. You would not see the dancers, only the lights if they were holding them. Describe the movement of the lights that you would see in the three areas of the carnival.

Diffusion – natural mixing for liquids and gases

Particles in liquids and gases move about randomly all the time.

If you carefully pour blackcurrant syrup into a glass of still water it forms a layer of syrup at the bottom. Leave it for the rest of the day and the random movements of the liquid particles **mix** the blackcurrant syrup and the water. At the end of the day the liquids are totally mixed. This process is called **diffusion**. Diffusion only happens in liquids and gases.

Liquids and gases mix together because the particles are moving about randomly. They can mix as the particles slide past each other.

Figure 4 Using blackcurrant syrup to demonstrate diffusion in a liquid.

A new smell spreads out

Liz was in the carnival procession. She was changing for the evening. She sprayed a new perfume deodorant all over herself – it was to be a night with lots of dancing. Sahera was next to her. She noticed the new perfume first and wanted to know what it was. It smelt really good. Then Jalminder, who was changing next to Sahera, noticed the smell as well and wanted to know the brand name. Finally Julia on the far side of the changing room asked where she could get some.

Inside the deodorant can, there is a gas under pressure that pushes the spray out. The can must be strong. There are many more particles hitting the inside than the outside.

3 What is the name of the process that spreads the smell?

4 How many seconds do you think it took to spread to Julia? (Use the second hand on a clock to help you guess.)

5 Draw a particles diagram to show how the perfume smell spreads through the air.

6 Draw a cartoon strip with sentences to explain how the pressure is greater inside the deodorant can than outside.

7 Make a list of all the pleasant smells that spread most easily through air.

8 'If a smell spreads really quickly, then it must be made up of small, fast-moving particles that diffuse through air easily.' Explain why this statement is true.

Remember

Use these words to complete the sentences.

**Brownian motion   smell   diffusion
mix   flow   forces   collide**

Liquids and gases are fluid, this means they ____1____. This happens because there are no ____2____ between the particles. The movement of the particles is called ____3____ _____.

Fluids will also ____4____ together. The process is ____5____. This is how a ____6____ spreads.

Gas pressure is caused when the particles in a gas ____7____ with the container they are in.

Watching changes

Have you ever seen a video running backwards? Sometimes you can't even tell that it's going the wrong way. Some scientists say that the only reason we can tell that time is passing is because everything in the world is getting more mixed together.

If you leave a bucket of **water** out in the garden for a long period of time, it doesn't stay **pure**. You don't even have to do anything to it.

At first, the water from the bucket starts to **evaporate** and makes a **mixture** with the **air**. **Acid rain** and other things fall into the water and dissolve in it to make a **solution**. If you wanted to use the water now, you would have to use **distillation** to make it pure again.

As the water continues to evaporate over time and more rain falls, the solution becomes more **concentrated**. Particles of dust from **weathered rock** and bits of earth blow into the bucket. Little organisms like algae and bacteria will be carried into the bucket on the earth and will live on the **salts** in the water. Plants like grasses or moss may take root on or near the bucket where the soil is moist.

With things to eat in the water – like the algae and bacteria – insects and snails will move into the bucket and use it as somewhere to live. They will **filter** the living things out of the water and eat them. Then larger animals – perhaps even a frog – will turn up to live off the smaller creatures.

The **metal** bucket will also be affected by the air and water. If it is made from iron, it will soon begin to **rust**. It will change colour from a silvery-grey colour to a red-brown, and the surface will become flaky, making it easier for the moss to grow.

If a video of these events was run backwards, nobody would be fooled into thinking it was running forwards.

Science uses the word **entropy** to describe this steady process of mixing up.

Questions

1 When you read the passage, does it make pictures appear in your head like a video clip? That's understanding!

   Draw four 'stills' pictures from your 'video'.

2 Write down the meaning of all the words which are given in the passage above in bold text. (Count weathered rock as one thing and acid rain as one thing.)

3 Make a list of all the words given in the passage in bold which have six letters or more. Learn to spell them by the Look – Say – Cover – Write method.

4 Write a passage to describe the gradual changes you would see where you live over a period of time.

Alchemists

Alchemists invented chemistry – in fact the words are very similar. Alchemists disguised science as magic to appear mysterious and clever. Kings employed alchemists because they thought they would turn ordinary metal into gold. There have been famous alchemists all through history.

Maria Hebraea (1st Century AD) was an expert alchemist whose distilling techniques are still in use today.

Zosimus (3rd Century AD) was a Greek alchemist who believed that all substances were composed of the four elements of nature: Fire, Water, Air and Earth. He collected together all knowledge on Khemia, as it was then known. Much of the knowledge was destroyed by the Christians who burned the library in Alexandria in 391 AD.

Geber (8th Century AD) was an Arabian alchemist who lived in what we now know as Iraq. He popularised the idea of the Philosopher's Stone which would combine the mercury and sulphur to make gold. He also distilled strong acid from vinegar and believed that metals were made up of mercury and sulphur in varying proportions.

Paracelsus (16th Century AD) invented the word alcohol from the arabic 'al-kohl'. Paracelsus strongly believed in spiritual alchemy. He said that the purpose of alchemy was not to make gold, but to cure diseases.

Isaac Newton (17th Century AD)

One of the last well known alchemists was Isaac Newton. As well as studying physics and maths, Newton spent much of his time on alchemy. It is said that Newton was not the first scientist of the age of reason, but he was the last of the magicians. Documents show the inspiration for his work on light and gravity came from his obsession with alchemy. It is even suggested that Newton did succeed in making lead turn into gold . . .

Nanotechnology

In Star Trek Voyager, Seven of Nine has nanoprobes in her body. These control her body systems, keep her really healthy and give her superhuman abilities.

Nanotechnology is a new idea about making really tiny machines. The machines are so small that you can't see them without a microscope. The idea was first proposed by Richard Feynman, who was a brilliant scientist. He proved that if you could work with single particles of matter you could print the whole 24 volumes of the Encyclopaedia Britannica on the head of a pin. The letters could be 30 particles wide and still fit on the pin-head.

Since then, people have worked to develop tiny motors and gears to make tiny machines. They are trying to make machines that are so small they could travel through your bloodstream and repair parts of your body.

Other people are very worried about the nanobots getting 'out of control'. They think the robots will degrade materials until a world made of 'grey goo' is all that remains.

Nanotechnology is a growing science. It will provide lots of exciting jobs for young people with imagination.

Activity

Imagine a world in which microscopic robots are sent into the human body with the mission of detecting cancer cells, destroying them, and turning them into waste products. Then imagine similar robots in the hands of a sinister force that wants to turn an entire continent into grey dust.

1 You must decide if nanotechnology is a good thing to develop.

Is the benefit of curing diseases, like cancer, worth the risk of technology falling into the wrong hands and being misused?

Do you think that nanotechnology could be beneficial to enough people for it to be worthwhile to continue, despite the risks? These are the sort of *ethical* decisions that scientists have to make.

Write a few sentences to explain your decision.

Energy and fuels

Some people don't eat meat. They think it's wrong to eat animals. But what about eating fruit and vegetables such as potatoes?

We get energy from our food so that we can grow, move and keep warm. Plants need energy, too. Their leaves get energy from sunlight. They can then store energy for the future. For example, a potato is an energy store made by a potato plant.

When a potato is planted underground it provides the fuel for a new plant to grow.

Potatoes provide fuel for people, too. But that means that when you eat a potato it will never provide energy for a new potato plant to grow. **You** get the energy instead.

Activity

1 Where does a potato plant get energy from as it grows in a field?

2 Where do people get energy from?

3 Do you think that it is wrong to eat animals?

4 Do you think that it is wrong to eat the energy stores of plants, such as potatoes?

5 If we didn't eat animals or plants, what could we eat?

Temperature changes

Temperature is a variable that we can measure using thermometers.

Figure 1

'Hungry?' said Chris.

'You bet,' I said.

'OK, it won't be too long. We've just got to let the oven warm up, then the pizza will start to cook.'

'How long will that be?' I asked.

'It'll be a few minutes before the oven gets to 180°C. Then it will be hot enough and we can put the pizza in. It'll just need 20 minutes more after that.'

Temperature is something that changes. It is also something that we can measure. It is a **variable**.

Every measurement of temperature is not just a number but has a **unit** as well. When we say the temperature of the oven is 180°C, the number is 180 and the unit is °C, which stands for **degrees Celsius**.

We can change the temperature of something by heating it. The hot oven heats the pizza. The pizza might have a temperature of only 4°C when we put it into the oven, but it rises to 180°C.

When we take the pizza out of the oven its temperature starts to fall. If we leave it for too long it falls to the same temperature as the room around it. Room temperature is usually about 20°C. Though the temperature of the pizza is as warm as the air in the room, it's not so good to eat and we say it's 'gone cold'.

Measuring temperature

We can use **thermometers** to measure temperature. A thermometer is a **measuring instrument**. The most common kind of thermometer is a glass tube with a **bulb** at one end. Inside the bulb is a liquid. This is usually **alcohol** or **mercury**. When the temperature of the liquid increases, it **expands** and spreads along the inside of the tube. The tube has markings along the outside, and the main markings are numbered. The markings and numbers are called a **scale**. We can look at the numbers to find out the temperature in °C.

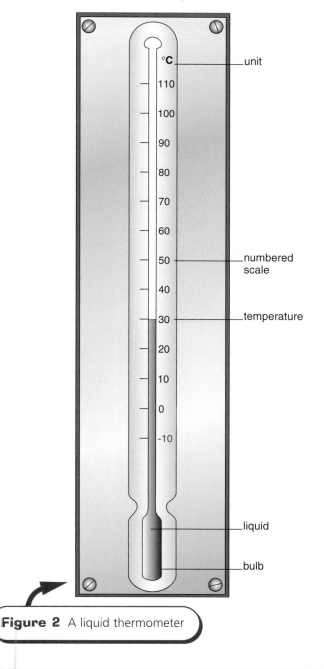

Figure 2 A liquid thermometer

1 What unit do we use for measuring temperature?

2 What measuring instrument do we use for measuring temperature?

3 What liquids might you find inside a thermometer?

4 What happens to the liquid in the thermometer when the temperature increases?

5 How much did the temperature of the pizza change while it was in the oven?

6 How much does the temperature of a pizza change when it cools from 180°C to 20°C?

7 Draw a thermometer scale in your book. Go from 0°C to 100°C. Use 1 cm to equal 10°C. Mark the freezing point of water on your scale.

8 Mark the boiling point of water on your scale.

9 Mark today's temperature on your scale.

Remember

Use these words to complete the sentences.

**degree Celsius   bulb   scale
mercury   measuring   variable
thermometer   expands   alcohol
unit**

Temperature is a changing quantity called a ____1____. We use a ____2____ instrument called a ____3____ to measure it. The ____4____ for measuring temperature is called a ____5____. A thermometer has a ____6____ that contains a liquid such as ____7____ or ____8____. The liquid ____9____ when the temperature increases. The liquid moves along a ____10____ on the thermometer.

Energy from the Sun

Solar cells and the leaves of plants take energy from the light of the Sun. The Sun is also the source of other energy resources.

Figure 1 The energy of the Sun creates winds. We can use **wind generators** to provide electricity.

Figure 4 Plants provide the energy that animals need to live and grow. Cows eat grass nearly all day long so that they have enough energy to live.

Figure 5 Food – an energy resource provided by the light of the Sun.

Figure 2 For some homes, **solar cells** provide electricity, like batteries do. But they only work when light is shining on them. The light provides the energy to make them work. The solar cells transfer the energy so that we can use it for heating and working machinery.

Figure 6 Trees use energy from the light of the Sun to grow. We can use the trees as fuel. Fuel made from material that has been alive, like trees, is called a **biomass energy resource**.

Figure 3 Leaves and solar cells have large flat surfaces. They absorb light and gain energy. **Photosynthesis** is the name we give to the way plants use energy from light to build up their energy stores. Plants need energy to grow and to get water from their roots.

Figure 7 In some places in forests and swamps, layers of dead trees and other plants build up. Eventually, the layers might be buried by mud or sand.

Figure 8 This coalminer is deep underground, digging out coal formed from layers of plants that died millions of years ago.

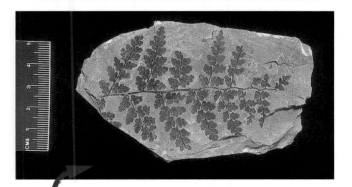

Figure 9 Sometimes you can still find signs of the old plants in the coal. This is a **fossil** of a leaf that grew a very long time ago – before there were even any dinosaurs. Coal is a **fossil fuel**.

Questions

1 **a)** Where does a cow get its energy from?

   b) Where do you get your energy from?

2 **a)** Name two similarities between solar cells and leaves.

   b) Name two differences.

3 We could burn dried sewage as a fuel.

   a) What kind of energy resource is sewage?

   b) Do you think that this would be a good idea?

4 Why is coal called a fossil fuel?

5 **a)** Make a list of as many different energy resources as you can. Here are two to get you started: food, coal.

   b) Can you think of any energy resources that are not created by the energy of sunlight?

Remember

Complete the sentences by unscrambling the letters.

There are many kinds of energy resource. Plants carry out <u>TEST SHINY HOOPS</u> to build up their energy stores from the light of the Sun. Our <u>DOFO</u> is the energy resource that our bodies need.

We can burn plants. They provide a <u>I SOB SAM</u> energy resource. Plants that have been buried in layers underground can turn into coal. Coal is a <u>LOSS IF</u> fuel.

Batteries and <u>ALSO R</u> cells provide energy for electric circuits. The energy of the Sun also creates winds. We can use wind <u>RONG EATERS</u> to take advantage of this energy resource.

Electric choices I

We can use different energy resources to generate electricity. Some of the resources are renewable, some are not.

Renewable and non-renewable

Have you flicked a switch today? What happened? You'll probably flick some more before the day is over. Lights will go on and off, music and voices will start and stop. You'll enjoy the power.

But it's not all good news. Electricity is generated in power stations. Most power stations burn a lot of fuel – usually coal, oil or gas. These **fossil fuels** come from under the ground. One day the fuel under the ground will all be used up and there is no way to replace it. It is **non-renewable**. Also, burning fuels produces pollution. Gases go into the atmosphere where they can do harm.

Some energy resources are **renewable**. They will not run out. For example, as long as the Sun shines there will be winds in the Earth's atmosphere. Energy resources like wind don't pollute the atmosphere.

So it's our choice. We could carry on just as we are now – flicking switches whenever we want for light, warmth and entertainment. Or we could stop using electricity. Or we could use more electricity that is generated without burning fuels. Some of the choices are shown below and on the next page.

let's go crazy!

We stop using electricity?

We use electricity much as we want, using the cheapest energy resources, and don't think about the future?

We use several kinds of energy resources, including renewable resources, so that we make less pollution and fossil fuels last longer?

Figure 1 Which is your choice?

Energy resource	Renewable or non-renewable	Pollution level	Advantages
Coal is a fossil fuel made from plants that were buried many millions of years ago. Burning coal produces steam that turns **turbines** and **generators** in power stations.	Non-renewable	Very high	There is quite a lot of coal still in the ground, for now. It is quite cheap to use in very large power stations.
Gas is a fossil fuel, used in power stations.	Non-renewable	High	Cheap to use in large and medium-sized power stations.
Oil is another fossil fuel, used in power stations.	Non-renewable	Very high	Moderately cheap to use in large and medium-sized power stations.
Biomass – plant and animal waste material, including dead plants and sewage.\n\nBurning biomass produces direct heating. Or it can provide fuel for power stations.	Renewable	Quite high (but by always growing new plants a lot of pollution is taken back out of the air).	If we grow plants to replace ones that are used then biomass energy need never run out.
Wind – energy of moving air used to turn wind turbines and generators.	Renewable	Low – but wind generators can spoil the peace of the countryside.	Wind will blow for billions of years. There is no burning involved.
Solar cells – energy straight from the Sun.	Renewable	Very low – they don't produce any direct pollution.	Energy from the Sun will last for billions of years. There is no burning involved.

Table 1

Electric choices II

We all want the benefits that come with having a big energy supply. We want the light, heat, transport and entertainment. But there are problems as well.

Problem 1

Fossil fuels are our main energy resource. The first problem with fossil fuels is that they produce pollution when we burn them. There are different kinds of pollution. In cities they can create **smog**, which is smoky fog. They can also harm the countryside by making **acid rain**. Acid rain damages trees and buildings, and kills fish in lakes. Burning fossil fuels also produces a lot of **carbon dioxide**. That goes into the Earth's **atmosphere** – the air that surrounds the planet. The change in the atmosphere makes the Earth warmer, causing **global climate change**. This will go on for as long as we burn the fossil fuels. We don't know what the final results will be.

Problem 2

The second problem with fossil fuels is that they are non-renewable.

Fossil fuels are the remains of plants and animals that lived in the sunshine millions of years ago. These remains have been buried in rock and preserved. We use oil rigs and coal mines, for example, to get them out of the ground.

Figure 1 City smog is made by burning fossil fuels.

Figure 2 One kind of pollution from burning fuel can come back to ground level as acid rain. It can damage trees and kill fish.

The supply of coal, oil and gas will not last much longer unless we do not use them so much. Future generations of people will have no fossil fuels to use.

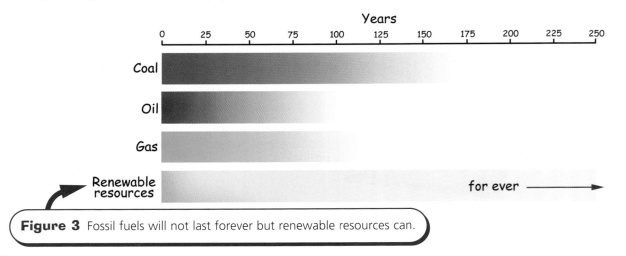

Figure 3 Fossil fuels will not last forever but renewable resources can.

Every choice has its problems. None of the ways of generating electricity is perfect. Different generating methods should be compared for:

- how much they cost
- how reliable the supply would be
- how much they damage the environment.

Energy source for generating electricity	Advantage	Disadvantage
Coal	Cheap to run	Acid rain and global climate change
Oil	Cheap to run, quick to start up	Acid rain and global climate change
Gas	Very cheap to run, very quick to start up	Global climate change
Nuclear	Cheap to run	Long-term danger of waste leaking into the environment. Catastrophic accidents
Hydro-electric	No fuel costs. Quick to start up. Leisure use of lakes	Very expensive to build. Destroys countryside
Wind	No fuel costs	Takes up a lot of space: noisy and ugly. Unreliable supply
Wave	No fuel costs	Expensive to build and unreliable supply
Solar – electric	Can be installed anywhere. Small generators possible. Low running costs	Expensive. Only works during the day

Questions

1 How would you cope without electricity? Write down three things that you would have to give up.

2 Look back at Spread 3.3. How many different energy resources are mentioned? Sort them into two lists: renewable and non-renewable.

3 Why do we use more coal than wood in power stations?

4 What are the disadvantages of using **a)** coal? **b)** wind generators?

5 Which of the energy resources in Table 1 on page 35 are fossil fuels? Where do they come from? What are the harmful effects of burning them?

6 Are we being selfish in using up fossil fuels now and not leaving them for future generations of people?

7 Are we being selfish in burning fossil fuels and changing the atmosphere, when we don't know what effects this will have on the future of the world's climate?

Remember

Use these words to complete the sentences.

resources   non-renewable   renewable   generate   fossil

Oil, coal, gas, biomass, wind, moving water and solar cells are all energy ____1____. We can use them all to ____2____ electricity. Oil, coal and gas are ____3____ fuels. They are made from dead plants and animals that became buried in the ground many millions of years ago. We are digging up these fuels very quickly and they cannot be replaced. They are ____4____. Biomass, wind, water and solar cells are all ____5____ energy resources. They will not run out.

Sunshine

Have you ever wondered where all our energy comes from? If you think the answer is the Sun, you would be nearly correct. Except for nuclear energy and geothermal energy, all our energy *does* come from the Sun. Geothermal energy comes from radioactive materials heating rocks in the Earth's crust.

A few years ago there was a total **eclipse** of the Sun that was visible in Devon and Cornwall. The temperature dropped and animals started to get ready for the night even though it was only 11 a.m. The most unusual thing was how nervous people felt as the Sun disappeared, and how happy they felt when the Sun reappeared.

The Sun is our nearest **star**. It is at the centre of our Solar System. Early civilisations, like the Incas who lived in Peru in South America around 500 years ago, worshipped the Sun – it was their god. All of us worship the Sun to some extent. On a sunny day we feel happier and play in the sunshine. Can you imagine the Sun being switched off? What would happen to life on Earth?

At the centre of the Sun is its **core**. This core takes up about one tenth of the Sun's radius. Scientists think the temperature in the core is about 15 million °C. The visible surface of the Sun is called the **photosphere**. This is the part that sends us all our heat and light. The temperature at the surface is only 6000 °C!

Sunspots are darker areas which appear on the surface in cycles of about 11 years. Sunspots are a little cooler than the surrounding photosphere. They give rise to bright eruptions called **flares** on the Sun's surface. These flares send charged particles towards the Earth which can cause interference with radio communications.

During solar eclipses, a bright red region called the **chromosphere** can be seen. Normally the Sun's light is too bright for us to see the chromosphere. It is a region of not very dense gas less than 100 km thick. The chromosphere gives rise to **prominences**. These are glowing gas jets ejected from the Sun to heights of over 300 000 km. Beyond the chromosphere is the **corona**. The corona, like the chromosphere, is only visible during a solar eclipse.

The Sun's fuel is hydrogen. We think of the Sun as a ball of fire, but that is totally wrong. If it was a ball of fire it would have lasted less than 50 years, but it's been there for 10 billion years. Sunshine is produced by **nuclear fusion**. This is when hydrogen nuclei are rammed together to form larger nuclei. During fusion, a little of the mass of the hydrogen fuel is converted to energy. Every second, the Sun loses over 4 million tonnes of mass which is transferred as energy. This energy provides the Earth's major energy source and is what keeps you alive.

Questions

1 Make a list of the words in bold and write their meanings next to them.

2 Write a *new* sentence using each word in the list.

3 Use the information to draw a cross-section through the Sun.

4 What happens here on Earth thanks to energy from the Sun? (To help you with this, think about what <u>wouldn't</u> happen if the Earth stopped receiving energy from the Sun.)

Scientists

Lyndsay Fletcher

Lyndsay Fletcher's favourite subjects at school were English and German. But there was something about science that offered a bit more of a challenge. She wanted to know how the world worked. So when she left school she went to university, in Glasgow, and studied Physics and Astronomy.

At university, Lyndsay did well. She went on to study further and became Doctor Lyndsay Fletcher – a world class expert on the Sun.

There are satellites up above the Earth, with names like SOHO and TRACE. The instruments on these satellites point towards the Sun, and they gather information about its hot outer layers and about its magnetism. Lyndsay works with the information that these satellites gather.

The Sun's surface makes huge energetic bursts called solar flares. They can affect satellites, radio broadcasts, power transmission and the health of astronauts. But so far nobody knows just how these flares work. Lyndsay is working on an idea that the Sun's magnetism can store energy, which is then released in bursts. As she says, 'these bursts or flares are important to humans and to technology in space, but the real reason I like doing my research is because it's such an interesting puzzle!'

Figure 1 Californian sunshine. People all around the world are interested in what Lyndsay has to say about how the Sun works. So she gets to travel to meet them, wherever they are. Lyndsay uses maths and computers to work out what's happening on the surface of the Sun.

Fuels

We can measure the energy values of different fuels.

Fuels provide energy when they burn. They heat their surroundings. We can use the heating effect to make fuels do work for us. In a car engine, air and a little bit of fuel get very, very hot. The fuel burns and it gets so hot that there is a small explosion. The explosion pushes a piston and that's what makes the wheels go round. Only small amounts of fuel burn at a time. Each small explosion doesn't last very long. But there are a lot of explosions, one after the other.

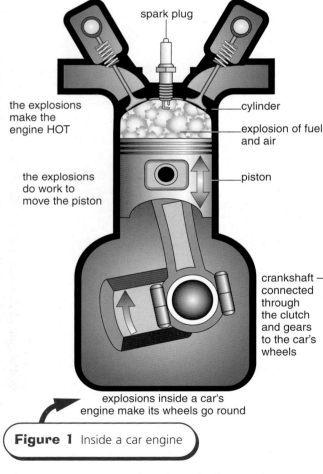

spark plug

the explosions make the engine HOT

cylinder

explosion of fuel and air

the explosions do work to move the piston

piston

crankshaft – connected through the clutch and gears to the car's wheels

explosions inside a car's engine make its wheels go round

Figure 1 Inside a car engine

Most cars use petrol as their fuel. Petrol comes from oil. That means that petrol is a fossil fuel. Some cars run on diesel which is also a fossil fuel. Cars can also use alcohol as a fuel. Some can even use **methane**, which is the name of the gas that we use as a fuel for gas cookers and gas fires.

Different fuels have different **energy values**. You can measure the energy value of a fuel by measuring how much it heats. It's possible to burn fuel and see how much it heats some water. To compare fuels in this way it's important to make **fair tests**. That means using the same amount of fuel for each test. It also means using the same amount of water.

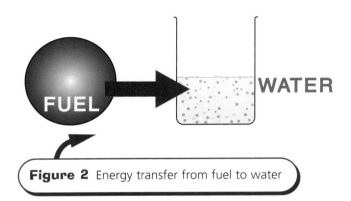

FUEL

WATER

Figure 2 Energy transfer from fuel to water

Units

We can measure the amount, or mass, of fuel in **grams** or **kilograms**. A kilogram is a thousand grams.

Water is a liquid, and we can measure the amount, or volume, of water in **millilitres**.

The unit of energy is called a **joule**, or J for short. Mega means a million of something, so a **megajoule** is a million joules.

The energy value of fuel has a complicated unit. The energy value of coal is 35 megajoules per kilogram. That means that a kilogram of coal provides 35 megajoules of energy.

Fuel	Energy value in megajoules per kilogram
hydrogen	140
methane	52
petrol	48
coal	35
butter	34
sugar	17
wood	13

Table 1   The energy values of some fuels

This pile of coal, around 100kg, could provide 3500 megajoules of energy!

Figure 3

Remember

Use the words below to complete the sentences.

megajoule   joule   fair test   methane gram   millilitre   energy values kilogram

We can measure energy using a unit called a _____1_____. One million joules can also be called one _____2_____.

We can measure an amount (mass) of coal using a unit called a _____3_____ or a unit called a _____4_____.

We can measure an amount (volume) of water using a unit called a _____5_____.

_____6_____ is a fuel that many people use at home. We can compare the _____7_____ _____ of different fuels by seeing how much they heat water. We have to make sure that we carry out a _____8_____.

Questions

1 Which of the fuels in Table 1 can you use for your body?

2 Make a bar chart to show the energy values of different fuels. If you can, use a computer to help you with this.

3 What do you normally call 'methane' in everyday language?

4 Match up the units to the quantities that they measure:

energy   millilitre
amount (volume) of water   megajoule per kilogram
amount (mass) of coal   joule or megajoule
energy value of fuel   gram or kilogram

5 Which fuel in Table 1 has the highest energy value?

6 a) Copy and complete:

The energy value of hydrogen is _____ times as big as the energy value of coal.

b) How many joules are there in a megajoule?

c) How many grams would you expect there to be in a megagram?

Closer

You and the planet, 60 years from now

Figure 1 This could be you, 60 years from now.

What will the world be like 60 years from now? You won't be the same as you are now. And the world itself will have changed.

Nobody knows just how the world will change. But there are some things that we can predict. For example, if we keep on using oil and gas, as we do now, then they will be nearly all used up.

We know that when we burn fossil fuels they make carbon dioxide. Carbon dioxide in the atmosphere can change the Earth's climate. But nobody knows how much it will actually change.

Activity

1 Where do we get oil, gas and coal from? Why will we run out of these fuels?

2 Find out more about energy resources and climate change. Do an internet word search of UK websites. Try using some of the following keywords in your search:

   - renewable energy
   - fossil fuel
   - climate change
   - acid rain
   - solar energy
   - wind energy
   - Kyoto Treaty.

   Use your search results to help you with Question 3.

3 The exact effect of carbon dioxide on the Earth's climate is an area of 'scientific uncertainty'.

   - What does 'scientific uncertainty' mean?

- Some people say:
  A 'Burning fossil fuels has no effect on the world's climate.'
  Others say:
  B 'We must stop using fossil fuels so much.'
  What sort of people are more likely to make statement **A**? What about statement **B**?

- To find out what is going to happen we could just wait and see. Or we could do more scientific tests so that we understand more.
  Which of those options do you think is best? Explain why.

- What are these people doing about possible climate change?

**scientists   politicians   oil companies
teachers   you**

Reproduction

Opener Activity
Growing up

A new-born animal can only survive if it has enough food and water and the temperature and weather conditions are good. The time between an egg being fertilised and a baby being born is known as the **gestation period**.

The table below shows the gestation period of some common animals.

Animal	Average gestation period (days)
Camel	406
Cat	62
Cow	280
Chimpanzee	237
African elephant	640
Fox	52
Horse	337
Human	266
Mouse	21
Rabbit	32
Sheep	148

There are three types of animal breeding patterns:

- continuous or opportunist
- short day
- long day.

Look at the descriptions of the advantages of breeding in these ways and match the description to the type of breeder.

These breeders are found in countries where the weather doesn't vary very much and there is a constant supply of food. Many mammals in Africa are this type of breeder.

These breeders mate in spring and summer. They are usually small mammals or birds with a short gestation period. This gives the young enough time to build up their strength to survive the winter or migrate to warmer environments.

These animals usually have a long gestation period. They mate during autumn, and give birth in the spring. This gives the young time to build up strength to survive the hard winter months.

Figure 1 (a) Continuous/opportunist – S. African impala (b) Long day – Australian Zebra finch (c) Short day – white tailed deer.

Questions

1 A mouse has a gestation period of about 21 days. Are they likely to be a continuous breeder or a different type of breeder?

2 Humans have a gestation period of about 266 days and babies can be born at any point in the year. What type of breeder does this make them?

3 Why is it important for short-day breeding animals to have a relatively short gestation period?

4 How does having a long gestation period help long-day breeding animals?

5 Work out approximately how many months each gestation period is for each animal. Assume that a month has 30 days.

Starting a new life

Male and female reproductive organs are very different.

Becoming a parent is a big responsibility. Looking after babies – feeding them, changing nappies and making sure that they are warm and safe – is a full-time job. A new life begins when a sperm cell from the father joins with an egg cell from the mother. This process is called **fertilisation**. In mammals it happens inside the female's body.

Lots of people get embarrassed when they are learning about or discussing their reproductive system. This is normal and it's the way that everyone feels. Our culture keeps its reproductive systems private as special places away from touch and sight. We have developed this approach over thousands of years, and we respect this way of doing things. As a result, we only know about our own type of reproductive system, male or female. We learn about the other type from books.

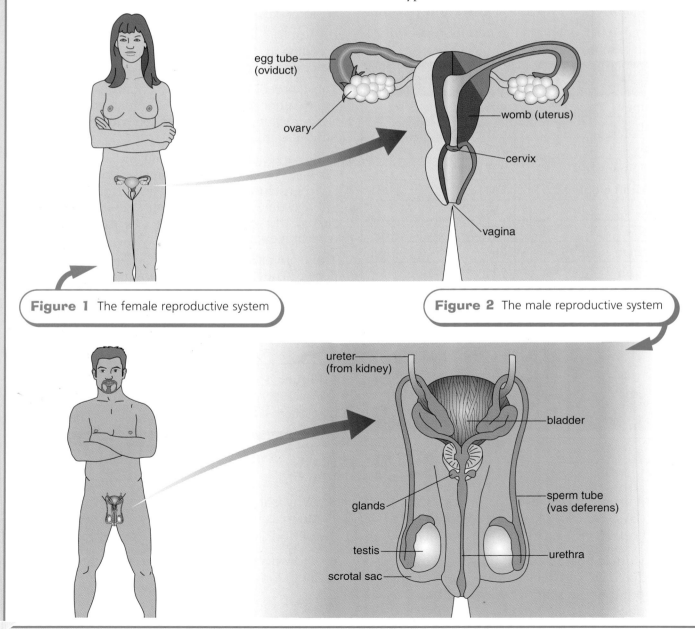

egg tube (oviduct)

ovary

womb (uterus)

cervix

vagina

Figure 1 The female reproductive system

Figure 2 The male reproductive system

ureter (from kidney)

bladder

glands

sperm tube (vas deferens)

testis

urethra

scrotal sac

Producing sperm and egg cells

Egg cells are made inside the **ovaries**. When a girl reaches puberty, her ovaries start to produce egg cells. In adults, one egg is released each month. In young girls the release of eggs can be irregular but it usually settles down once the girl has fully matured. The egg cell passes down the egg tube or **oviduct**. If it meets with a **sperm cell** and joins with it, fertilisation takes place and the egg can begin to divide. The fertilised egg will enter the **womb** (uterus) where it attaches itself to the wall of the womb. It may then continue to divide and grow into a baby, being born about nine months later.

Sperm cells are made in the man's **testis** (the plural is testes). Sperm cells are very sensitive to temperature. A man's body temperature is too high for sperm cells to live and reproduce so the testis hangs outside the body in a sac of skin – the **scrotal sac** or **scrotum**. When sperm cells are produced, they pass through the sperm tube or **vas deferens**. As they pass the glands underneath the **prostate gland**, fluids are added which keep the sperm cells alive. The sperm and the fluid together are known as **semen**.

Remember

Draw, label and learn the diagrams of the male and female reproductive systems.

Questions

1   Complete Table 1 below.

Name	Male or female?	What it does
oviduct	female	
	male	carries the sperm from the testes
	male and female	stores urine
prostrate gland		adds fluid to sperm to make semen
scrotal sac	male	
womb (uterus)		

Table 1

2   Where are the sperm produced in the male?

3   Where are the eggs produced in the female?

4   Why are the testes outside the male body in a sac of skin?

5   What is the name for the sperm and the fluid that keeps it alive?

6   How do the eggs get to the womb?

7   Make a list of all the words in bold in the text and learn their meanings.

8   Imagine having to look after a fragile thing, such as an uncooked egg, all day long. This is like caring for a baby. Write about how you would keep and protect it:

- on the journey to school
- during lessons
- at lunchtime and in the dinner queue
- when you are out at play.

Fertilisation

Fertilisation is the joining together of a sperm cell and an egg cell.

For fertilisation to happen, the sperm and egg must come into contact with each other. When people have sexual intercourse or 'make love' it allows the egg cell and the sperm cells to come into contact with one another. Sexual intercourse is not just about having babies. Men and women will have sexual intercourse for pleasure and for showing their love and commitment to their chosen partner.

During sexual intercourse, the man will become excited and his penis becomes stiff or erect. This happens because it fills with blood. When a woman becomes excited she produces a fluid that lubricates the vagina and the entrance to the vagina. The man's penis can be inserted into the vagina and moved in and out. This increases the pleasure for the man and woman and eventually the sperm are pumped into the vagina in the semen as the man ejaculates.

1 During sexual intercourse the man's penis becomes stiff. This is due to blood flowing into the penis.

2 When the woman becomes excited she produces a fluid in the vagina.

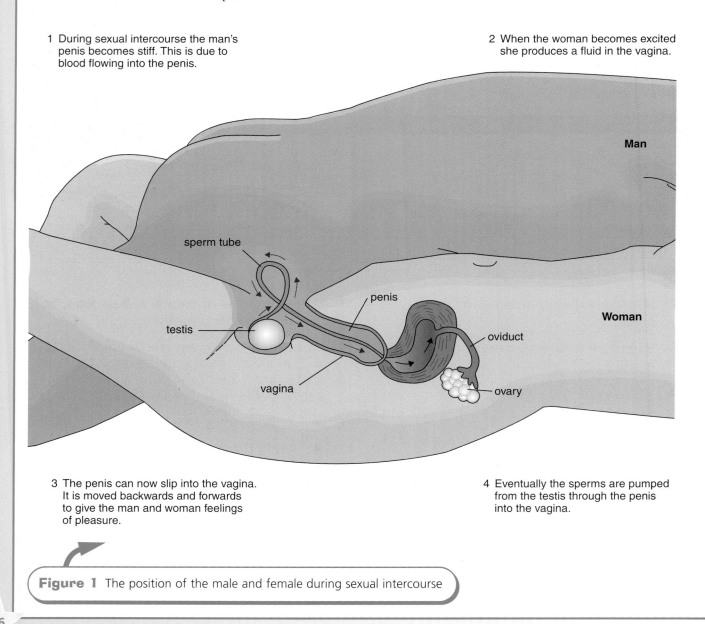

3 The penis can now slip into the vagina. It is moved backwards and forwards to give the man and woman feelings of pleasure.

4 Eventually the sperms are pumped from the testis through the penis into the vagina.

Figure 1 The position of the male and female during sexual intercourse

The sperm then swim from the vagina into the womb and eventually reach the oviduct. If there is an egg in the oviduct or womb it could be fertilised by a sperm and the woman will become pregnant. The fertilised egg will carry on down the oviduct and attach itself to the wall of the womb where it will eventually grow into a baby.

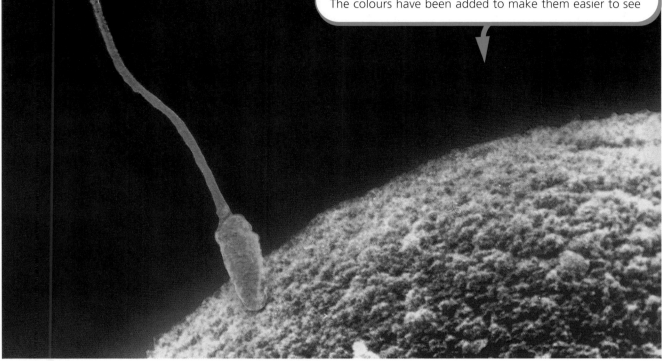

Figure 2 The egg is many times larger than the sperm. The colours have been added to make them easier to see

---

Questions

1 In what part of the female is sperm deposited?

2 How does the sperm get into the womb?

In a small group talk sensibly about the following things. You may feel more comfortable writing down your thoughts or discussing them with a close friend rather than speaking them aloud.

3 Do girls and boys act or think differently from each other? How? Why?

4 At what age do you think a person is ready to be a parent?

5 At what age do you think a person is ready to have sex?

6 What do you think are the qualities that a parent should have?

Remember

Use these words to complete the sentences below.

inside   fertilisation   intercourse   womb   swim   pregnant

Sexual ____1____ can make the female partner become ____2____. Sperm cells have to be able to ____3____ quite a long way ____4____ the female body for this to happen.

Successful ____5____ takes place in the oviduct or ____6____.

Growing in the womb

A single fertilised cell grows into a foetus inside the womb.

Once a fertilised egg settles in the wall of the womb, it begins to grow and develop into a baby. At first it is just a ball of cells and the cells divide just like the ones we discussed on page 6. After about 4 weeks it is possible to see the head area developing and some tiny stumps that will develop into the legs and arms.

Look at the series of photos and make a table in your book (Figure 1). In one column list the number of days after fertilisation and in the next column describe what the developing baby looks like. To begin with, the ball of cells is called an **embryo**. Once you can make out a head, arms, legs etc. and recognise what type of animal it is, we call it a **foetus**.

	Number of days after fertilisation	Description of embryo/foetus
	4	
	6	

Figure 1

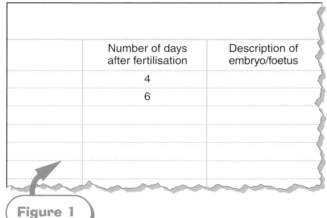

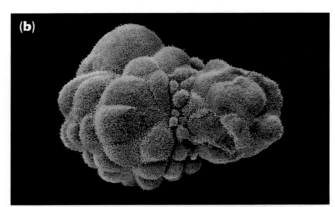

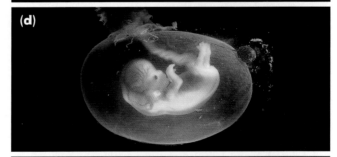

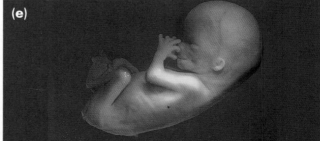

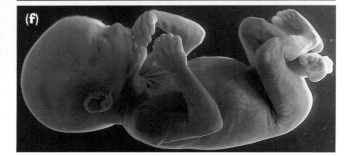

Figure 2 The developing foetus at: a) 4 days, b) 6 days, c) 28 days, d) 8 weeks, e) 15 weeks and f) 23 weeks

As the baby grows in its mother's womb, it needs to be fed, have a supply of oxygen, be protected from harmful infections and get rid of waste products. In order to do this a round disc-like organ – the **placenta** – grows on the surface of the womb. This is connected to the growing baby by a cord – the **umbilical cord**. The placenta is rich in blood vessels. The vessels have thin walls that allow oxygen and chemicals that the baby needs for energy and growth to pass from the mother's bloodstream into the baby's bloodstream. Any waste that the baby produces while it grows passes down the umbilical cord and across to the mother's bloodstream for the mother to get rid of. The placenta can stop some harmful substances and some bacteria from passing into the baby, but it cannot prevent everything. For example, alcohol can pass from the mother into the baby and this can harm the baby as it grows. Harmful chemicals in cigarette smoke also pass into the baby's bloodstream and can cause problems.

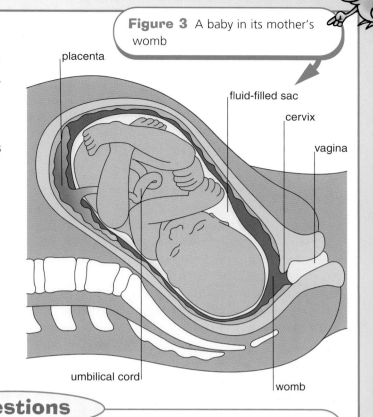

Figure 3 A baby in its mother's womb

placenta
fluid-filled sac
cervix
vagina
umbilical cord
womb

Questions

1   What is the difference between an embryo and a foetus?

2   After how many weeks do you think the embryo should be called a foetus?

3   How does the growing foetus get a supply of oxygen and nutrients?

4   Why does the growing foetus need the mother to eat sensibly and healthily during pregnancy?

5   Why are pregnant women advised not to smoke or drink during pregnancy?

6   The foetus sits inside a water-filled sac until it is ready to be born. How could this offer the foetus protection?

7   How is the embryo connected to the placenta?

8   What happens to this connection during birth and why is it no longer needed?

9   What materials are transferred from the baby's blood to the mother's blood in the placenta?

Remember

Use these words to complete the sentences below.

blood   umbilical   fertilised   mother's   baby's   placenta   oxygen   embryo   baby

The ____1____ egg cell grows and divides to form an ____2____. It grows inside the ____3____ womb.

The mother's ____4____ stream and ____5____ bloodstream are separate, but food and ____6____ can be transferred to the ____7____ via the ____8____. The connection is called the ____9____ cord.

Growing up is hard to do

Boys and girls go through a number of changes as they develop into adults. These changes happen at a stage called puberty.

Puberty

As you grow up, lots of things will happen to you. They won't all happen at the same time to everyone. This is perfectly normal. As your body grows and matures and you change from being a child to an adult you go through what is called **puberty**. Puberty can be a difficult time, but it's nothing to worry about.

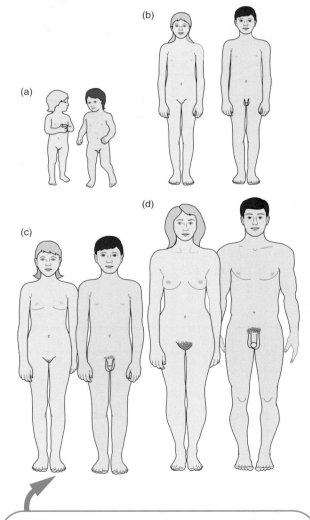

Figure 1 Some of the physical changes that take place when you grow up.

It is easy to see the physical changes that happen after you reach puberty (Figure 1). What is not so easy to see are the other changes that take place. Table 1 lists the sorts of changes that take place in boys and girls during puberty. Many of the changes are caused by **hormones**. Hormones are natural chemicals in your body that control things. Menstruation and growing body hair are caused by the presence of hormones.

Questions

1   How have you changed in the last four years?

2   What do you like and what do you not like about the changes?

3   How do you think you'll be different in five more years?

4   Do you think you'll like these changes?

5   What are the physical changes we can see in Figure 1 as we move from an adolescent to an adult?

6   What changes take place that we cannot see?

7   Exercise specialists say that young boys should not do a lot of heavy weight training before they are 16 years of age. Why do you think they give this advice?

8   Young girls often try to diet as they are going through puberty. What changes in their bodies might make young girls want to diet and why could it be harmful to them?

The menstrual cycle

Once a girl reaches adolescence, the time when she is changing from a girl to a woman, she begins to have periods. This is what we commonly call **menstruation**. Once an egg is

During puberty what happens to...	Boys	Girls
My body size?	The whole body begins to grow faster – a growth spurt – and your shoulders will broaden. You will also begin to develop more defined muscles.	The whole body begins to grow faster – a growth spurt. You will begin to get curves as your body deposits fat on your hips, buttocks and thighs.
My hair?	The hair on your head could become greasier and you will begin to grow body hair under your arms, on your chest, on your arms and legs and around your penis (pubic hair). You will also have an increase in growth of facial hair.	The hair on your head could become greasier and you will begin to grow body hair under your arms and around your vagina (pubic hair).
My voice?	Your voice becomes deeper and your larynx (Adam's Apple) gets larger.	Your voice won't change much.
My skin?	You could develop 'spots' or mild acne. If it gets bad, see your pharmacist or doctor.	You could develop 'spots' or mild acne. If it gets bad, see your pharmacist or doctor.
My reproductive organs?	Your testes will grow larger and start producing sperm. Your penis will grow larger and may get slightly darker.	You will begin to grow breasts (mammary glands), your ovaries will begin to produce eggs and you will start to menstruate (have periods).

Table 1

released, the womb prepares to receive it. To do this the wall of the womb thickens. The lining of the womb has a rich supply of blood vessels. If a fertilised egg does not reach the womb and attach to the lining, the body knows that the lining is not needed. It breaks down and is passed out of the body through the vagina. This process is controlled by two hormones, **progesterone** and **oestrogen**.

In young girls just reaching puberty, their period may be irregular but as they grow older it should settle down and happen once every 28–30 days. The egg is released on or around day 14. The first day of bleeding in a woman is day 1 of the period.

Girls may begin to have periods at any age from about 9–17, usually around the age of 12 or 13. Lots of things can affect exactly when a girl's period will first begin such as her diet, overall health, amount of exercise, weight and genes (see page 83).

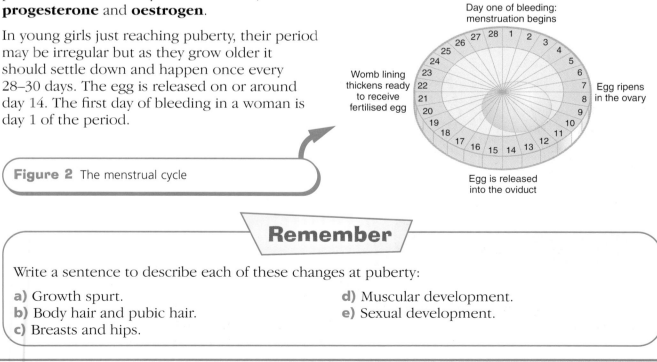

Figure 2 The menstrual cycle

Remember

Write a sentence to describe each of these changes at puberty:

a) Growth spurt.
b) Body hair and pubic hair.
c) Breasts and hips.
d) Muscular development.
e) Sexual development.

The problem page

Teenage magazines often have a problem page. They employ an 'agony aunt' or 'uncle' to try and solve your problems. Teenagers often moan about their parents not understanding what it is like growing up, but do remember they have also gone through what you're going through, even if it was some time ago!

Try putting yourself in the place of a parent or agony aunt/uncle. Read the teenagers' problems below and try to give them good, sensible advice. You may need to think back to some of the science you've learned about what happens when you grow up in order to help or reassure them. Write your replies in the form of letters to the teenagers.

Teenage problem 1

DEAR PROBLEM PAGE
I DON'T KNOW WHAT'S GOING ON. I AM A BOY OF 12 YEARS OF AGE. THE PROBLEM IS THAT EVERY TIME I OPEN MY MOUTH, MY VOICE SEEMS TO SQUEAK. ONE MINUTE IT'S HIGH PITCHED, THE NEXT VERY LOW. IT'S DIFFICULT FOR ME TO ANSWER QUESTIONS IN CLASS BECAUSE I THINK THE OTHERS WILL MAKE FUN OF ME. CAN YOU HELP ME AND LET ME KNOW WHAT'S GOING ON?

WORRIED OF WANDSWORTH

Teenage problem 2

Dear problem page
It's just not fair! I'm 14 and I haven't had my first period yet. I must be a freak. All my friends say they've had loads. Am I really a freak? Will I ever have a period?

Depressed of Derby

Teenage problem 3

Dear problem page

My mother is pregnant and I am worried. I don't see how a baby can survive inside her. I know that we all need oxygen to live and food to help us grow, including babies! What I don't understand is how the baby will get these if it's inside my mum. Can you please explain what is going on?

Confused of Clacton

Squeek!

Teenage problem 4

Dear problem page
My mother keeps on at me about how often I wash my hair. The trouble is I think it is greasy. It never used to be like this and there is no way that I am going to school with hair like that. She keeps shouting at me in the morning to hurry up in the shower. It wouldn't be so bad but she takes twice as long as me. If I could only give her a reason why I take so long then it wouldn't be so bad. Can you help?

Annoyed of Andover

Teenage problem 5

Dear problem page
When I have a shower after P.E., I find it difficult because I am beginning to grow some hair under my arms and around my private parts. Is this normal? (I am 12 years of age.) I thought that only adults grew hair on their body, surely I am too young for this. My friends point and snigger but am I right that this will also happen to them?

Shy of Sheffield

Teenage problem 6

Dear problem page
My friends have told me that kissing and cuddling can make a girl pregnant. I'm not certain that it does. I know that fertilisation has to take place because I remember hearing something about it in my science lesson. I wasn't listening in class so I didn't hear the rest. I'm too embarrassed to go back and ask my science teacher as she will think I'm an idiot. Can you help me and explain what fertilisation is?

Dreamer of Darlington

Remember

Design the front page of a leaflet for unhappy people of your age. The title of the leaflet is 'Share your concerns; everybody has problems growing up'.

Closer

If a woman is unable to produce eggs or a man cannot produce enough sperm they are said to be infertile. Infertility treatment is not a new idea. The following timeline shows how infertility treatment has progressed over the centuries. Artificial insemination means introducing male sperm into the female's oviduct without sexual intercourse taking place.

A 14th century Arab people may have used artificial insemination on horses.

B 1777 Italian priest began experiments with artificial insemination of reptiles.

C 1785 First attempts at human artificial insemination by John Hunter – a baby is born the same year.

D 1945 Early reports of donor insemination published in the British Medical Journal (BMJ).

E 1955 Four successful pregnancies using previously frozen sperm.

F 1969 Human fertilisation *in vitro* is achieved for the first time.

G 1978 Birth of Louise Brown, the first 'test tube' baby born as a result of IVF.

H 1992 Rosanna della Corte gives birth to a son, Riccardo, at the age of 62.

I 1996 The birth of Dolly the sheep, the first cloned mammal.

J 2001 Teams in the US and Italy announce that they are working on producing the first human clone.

K 2002 Claims are made that three human cloned pregnancies are taking place, two in Russia and one in 'an Islamic country'.

Activity

1   Using the dates in the timeline, find out what else was happening in this country and across the world. Draw some parallel timelines to show what you have found out.

CHAPTER 5

Solutions

Opener Activity
The case for using solutions

Blood plasma

Blood cells are suspended in a salty solution called blood plasma. The plasma carries the food from digestion round your body and takes the waste products away from your organs.

Hair gel

Hair gel changes its nature when you use it. It comes as a clear liquid, but then changes to a solid to keep your style perfectly in place.

Rubber solution

When you mend a puncture, the glue you use to stick the patch on is rubber solution. Rubber doesn't dissolve in water – if it did our tyres would be useless in the rain!

Suntan oil

The Sun produces harmful ultra-violet rays, and skin needs protection. We use creams and oils that are solutions of active ingredients that we can safely spread on our skin.

Questions

1 Do gases like carbon dioxide have the same dissolving rules as solids?

2 What liquids are there other than water that will do dissolving?

3 What actually happens when hair gel sets?

4 Apart from the protection it gives – what is different about a factor 30 sun tan oil compared to factor 5?

Good solutions

When a solid disappears into a liquid, a mixture called a solution is made. The solid that dissolves is called a solute and the liquid is a solvent.

Water dissolves many substances, including oxygen. Fish living in water can breathe using this oxygen. But water does not dissolve everything. If it did, rain would be a worse problem than it is.

Figure 1 This is what could happen if building materials dissolved in the rain!

When substances dissolve, the **solution** is transparent (see-through). If it is not transparent, it is not a real solution. These non-transparent liquids are called **suspensions** – they are tiny pieces of solids mixed up in a liquid.

If you want a substance like jelly to dissolve faster, use hot water and cut the jelly into small pieces. A higher temperature and a bigger surface area speed up dissolving.

Questions

1 **a)** Write down the names of some substances you know that dissolve in water.

   b) Next to their names, write the colour of the solution they make.

2 Make a list of drinks that are transparent. Put a heading 'solutions' above this list.

3 Make a list of drinks that are not transparent. Put 'suspensions' at the top of this list.

Concentrate on the job

Tom has a Saturday job. But he has made some silly mistakes.

'On my first day I had to make black coffee. I only know about instant coffee, but this was real coffee. I put one spoonful in the cup and added water. It turned out really weak and the coffee bits did not dissolve.

The manager told me the right way to make it. You pour boiling water on to the ground coffee. You filter the liquid that comes through. The boiling water dissolves the coffee taste out of the ground up coffee and the rest stays in the filter. You need to use a lot of ground coffee. There is less coffee taste in ground coffee than in instant coffee.

Figure 2 Making jelly

Figure 3 Tom in trouble at the café

Also, I adjusted the 'Coke' machine all wrong – too much syrup and not enough fizzy water in the mixture. People moaned about how concentrated the taste was.'

A **concentrated solution** has more **solute** (dissolved solid) in the **solvent** (liquid that does the dissolving).

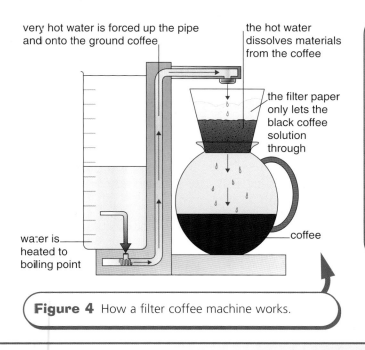

very hot water is forced up the pipe and onto the ground coffee

the hot water dissolves materials from the coffee

the filter paper only lets the black coffee solution through

water is heated to boiling point

coffee

Figure 4 How a filter coffee machine works.

Questions

4   Some people like 'weak' tea. How can you tell if it is weak?

5   If you make a thermos flask of instant coffee, you use much more coffee powder than you would for a mugful. Explain why.

6   Draw particle pictures of strong and weak solutions. If it was a coloured solute, how would the colours be different?

7   Devise a test to find out how much salt will dissolve in 100 cm³ of cold water. Write step-by-step instructions.

The difference between melting and dissolving

Dissolving needs *two* substances – a solute and a solvent.
E.g.: sugar and black coffee
        tea bag and water
        nail varnish and nail varnish remover

Melting needs only *one* substance.
E.g.: ice cubes in water
        butter in a frying pan
        ice cream on a hot day.

Remember

Match the words with the spaces.

**solute   solution   concentration
hot   solvent   powder**

A solid ____1____ dissolves in a ____2____ to make a mixture called a ____3____ . If the solute is a ____4____ or the solvent is ____5____ then the dissolving happens faster. The amount of solute in a solution is called the ____6____ .

Picture solutions

Some solids will dissolve in liquids – their particles join the random jumble. A solution is formed. It does not have the same properties as a pure substance.

Flash! The photographer's shutter opens for a sixtieth of a second and the glamorous image is captured.

Figure 1

High quality photographs still use a hundred-year-old method to make the picture. The film has caught only the faintest of images on tiny crystals of a light sensitive chemical. A wet chemical process involving several **solutions** then needs to be carried out before you can view the image.

Figure 2 Mata diluting the chemicals she needs to develop her photographs.

Mata is in charge of processing the photos.

She takes the film out of the camera and 'develops' it in a solution that makes the image much darker. Mata must dilute the chemicals to the correct **concentration**. She must also make sure that the temperature of the solution is right. She has to be careful. If the image gets too dark, the picture will be ruined.

The developer is washed from the picture and the image is 'fixed'. All the light sensitive material gets **dissolved** out of the film. The film is used to make lots of prints.

The 'fixer' solution needs changing every day – not because the chemicals have been used up, but because the solution has become **saturated** with the light sensitive material out of the film.

This material contains silver and is recycled because it is expensive to buy.

Questions

1 Mata uses two solutions. What do they do?

2 Why does Mata dilute the chemicals?

3 Which solution has to be changed every day? Explain why.

4 Why is the fixer recycled?

5 **a)** What is the solute for the fixer solution?

   b) What is the solvent for the fixer solution?

6 If the developer solution is left out in an open flat dish, the volume gets less. Explain why.

7 What would that do to the strength of the solution?

8 What is a saturated solution?

9 Draw a particle picture of a saturated solution.

Complete solutions

- Dissolving takes place because the solvent particles break the forces between the particles of the solid and pull it apart.
- The solid gets dissolved layer by layer from the outside in.
- The solid gets split up into tiny particles and can't be seen.
- A concentrated solution has lots of solute particles in a certain volume. A dilute solution has few dissolved particles in a certain volume.

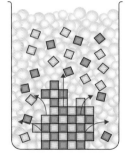

Key

 Water particles
Salt particles

a) The salt goes into the water. The water particles pull at the salt particles.

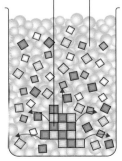

b) The salt particles are pulled away from each other. They mix with the water.

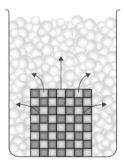

solid salt

liquid salt solution

c) Eventually nearly all the salt particles are pulled away from each other. When the last ones are pulled apart, the salt disappears.

Figure 3

A clean answer

Sahera wanted to remove sugary marks from her best jacket. She trained as an engineer so she knew lots of science. She knew

- hot water works better than cold as more solute dissolves in hot water
- there is a limit to how much solid will dissolve in a certain amount of solvent. The solvent becomes saturated after a while and can't dissolve any more
- water worked for sugar marks, but other stains needed different solvents
- it would be a disaster to use the wrong solvent
- to use ethanol (meths) to dissolve biro
- to use propanone to dissolve nail varnish.

Questions

10 Why did Sahera heat the water?

11 Why did Sahera keep changing the water?

12 What would Sahera use to remove biro ink marks?

13 Nail varnish remover will damage some fabrics. Write instructions for testing the fabric beforehand.

Remember

Fill in the spaces using the following words.

**solutions   dissolved   different
solute   concentration**

_____**1**_____ are a mixture of a _____**2**_____ and a solvent.

The _____**3**_____ is the amount of solute _____**4**_____ in a certain volume of solution.

Water dissolves many substances but oily materials need _____**5**_____ solvents.

Bends & sweets

Solids and gases both dissolve in liquids to form solutions. We are used to dissolving solids, but are perhaps less familiar with the idea of gases dissolving.

A lot of things that we see around us involve the dissolving of gases. For example:

- Steel rusts because oxygen dissolves in water.
- Fish have gills so they can breathe the dissolved oxygen from water.
- Drinks are fizzy because carbon dioxide is dissolved in them.

Deep breathing

When we breathe, air sweeps into our bodies and some of the oxygen gets absorbed through our lungs. The same volume of gas then sweeps out again.

We normally just consider the exchange of oxygen for carbon dioxide. But the air we breathe in is almost 80% nitrogen, and some of this gas dissolves in our blood as well. It does not react at all inside our bodies, but just gets carried round and round by the blood.

For scuba divers the dissolved nitrogen is very important. As they dive down, the air in the divers' lungs has to be under extra pressure to enable them to breathe. The extra pressure makes more of the nitrogen from the air dissolve in their blood plasma. When they surface, the nitrogen has to come out of their blood. If they dive too deep or swim to the surface too fast, the gas comes out of their blood like bubbles in a fizzy drink when the top is undone.

This condition – bubbles of nitrogen in the bloodstream – is called the 'bends'. It is very painful and very dangerous. In the worst cases, divers can die from it.

Sugar from reeds

Sugar for sweets, cakes and drinks comes mainly from a tropical reed called sugar cane. This cane grows to 6 metres in height in countries that are hot and wet. Sugar is a chemical called sucrose. Sugar cane sap contains up to 15% sucrose.

Sugar was introduced to Europe in the 11th Century. In the 16th Century, sugar was considered to be a luxury – a 1 kilogram bag of sugar would have cost £10 compared to 90p today.

Sugar used to be sold as big solid lumps from cone-shaped moulds. That's how Sugar Loaf Mountain in Rio de Janeiro in Brazil got its name. Sugar used to be wrapped in blue paper to disguise its yellow colour, but it's more pure now.

Making sugar

The following steps outline how raw sugar cane is turned into sugar.

- The sugar cane is shredded and washed with hot water to make a sugar cane juice.
- Lime (calcium oxide) is added and the mixture is filtered – this gently removes some of the impurities.
- The juice is then heated in a vacuum. The water boils at a lower temperature in the vacuum. If the mixture gets too hot, it will turn to toffee – the sugar molecules are decomposed by too much heat.

- This is continued until the solution is saturated, then small crystals of sugar, like icing sugar, are added.

- Big crystals grow around the little seed crystals.

- The big crystals are then separated from the syrupy juice by a machine called a centrifuge.

- The crystals formed are 98% sucrose.

Questions

1 'If you dive too deep or come up too quickly, your blood becomes like a shaken can of cola.' Explain why this happens.

2 What effect do the bends have on a diver? Use an encyclopaedia or the Internet to find out more about the bends.

3 What plant does sugar come from?

4 What conditions does sugar need to grow?

5 Why is the cane shredded before the juice is extracted?

6 Why is hot water used?

7 Why is the sugar cane juice heated in a vacuum?

8 What happens if the sugar cane juice gets too hot? What sort of chemical change is this?

9 Why are small sugar grains added to the saturated solution? If sugar crystallises slowly, what size of crystals will you get?

10 Draw a flow chart of the sugar-making process.

11 Draw a bar chart to display the solubility of these pure substances.

Substance	Table salt	Fungus killer (blue)	Washing soda	Drain cleaner	Fertiliser
Mass dissolved in 100 g of water at 20 °C	36 g	122 g	21 g	109 g	122 g

12 Celia took the temperature of a small amount of salol as it cooled.

Here are her results.
a) Plot a graph of her results.

b) What state was salol in at the start of the experiment (solid, liquid or gas)?

c) What state was salol in at the end of the experiment (solid, liquid or gas)?

d) What was the melting point of salol?

Time (mins)	Temp
0	70°C
1	60°C
2	50°C
3	44°C
4	46°C
5	46°C
6	46°C
7	40°C
8	34°C
9	28°C
10	23°C

Unscrambling liquids

Methods to separate solutes from solvents include crystallising, distilling, evaporating and chromatography.

Salt from sea water

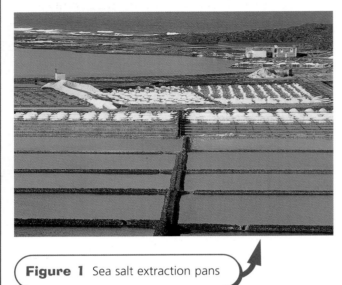

Figure 1 Sea salt extraction pans

70% of the surface of our planet is covered with water. Most of this water is undrinkable. It contains dissolved substances – mostly the material we know as table salt, but other materials as well.

Table salt is the chemical **sodium chloride**. In East Africa they make table salt from sea water. It is a two stage process. Firstly, sea water is pumped into a flat pond and left to **evaporate** in the Sun. The solution becomes more concentrated as the water evaporates. A substance called **calcium sulphate** comes out of sea water as a solid. This process is called **crystallising**. The calcium sulphate tastes nasty, so they do not want this in their table salt. Having separated out the nasty material, they pump the concentrated solution to a second pond. Here the hot Sun helps the water to evaporate so the sodium chloride crystallises out of solution. The sodium chloride (table salt) is dried in the Sun for the people to use.

Questions

1 What is the chemical name for 'table salt'?

2 What is the substance they don't want in their salt?

3 Why does this process work well in East Africa?

4 What is crystallisation?

Desalination

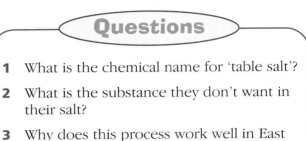

Figure 2 How to distil water in the lab

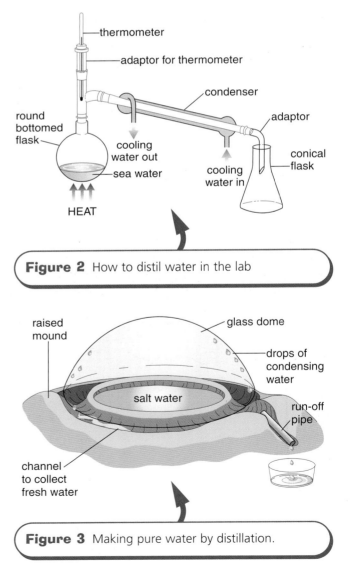

Figure 3 Making pure water by distillation.

You can 'unscramble' pure water from salt water.

The Ancient Greek Aristotle was the first person to notice this. He saw that when salt solution was boiled, the salt was left behind. The water escaped as steam. He knew that if you turned the steam back into water, it would be pure water.

In a hot dry country, a simple glass dome over a pool of salt water will make pure water (see Figure 3). The Sun evaporates the water. The vapour then condenses in the dome. A dome one metre across will produce 4.5 litres of pure water a day. This process is called **distillation**.

Alcohol from breath

An ink can be separated into the different dyes from which it is made. A sample of the ink is put on paper and placed in a solvent. The solvent soaks through the paper carrying the ink with it. The solvent carries the more soluble dyes up the paper faster than the less soluble ones (Figure 4). This is called **chromatography**.

Alcohol tests in police stations work in a similar way. The suspect's breath passes through a tube containing damp granules. Alcohol and other vapours dissolve differently in the granules, so they are separated. The breath then passes through a detector. This tells the police how much alcohol is in the suspect's body.

Figure 4 Separating the colours in ink by chromatography.

States change

Most materials can change state. Going from solid to liquid is called melting. Going from liquid to gas is called boiling or evaporating.

Breakfast! Mandy is a chocoholic. She likes to start the day with a hot chocolate drink and a piece of cake with chocolate on the top.

Melting

Figure 1

When the cook in Figure 1 melts the chocolate, it changes from being square chunks of chocolate bar to a brown liquid. It has to be heated on top of hot water for this to happen. The solid chocolate lumps change to a runny liquid.

When the chocolate is spread on the cake it solidifies as it cools. It remains in the shape it was spread into.

A 250 g bar of milk chocolate makes 250 g of melted chocolate. The weight does not get more or less when it melts but the melted chocolate has more energy.

Boiling

1   A hot chocolate drink needs hot milk. When you heat the milk in the pan it gets hotter because the hob **heats** it. The milk gains energy.

2   When it begins to boil, the milk forms lots of bubbles because the heat turns liquid milk into a gas. The gas makes the milk very frothy and it rises to the top of the pan.

3   It will spill out of the pan if you don't stop the milk being heated more. This is because the gas takes up more room than the liquid.

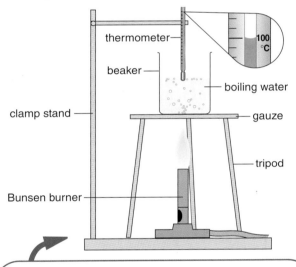

Figure 2 This is the correct way to take the temperature of boiling liquid. Don't let the thermometer touch the bottom of the beaker or the reading will be too high. Water boils at exactly **100°C**.

Questions

1   Ice tastes the same as water. Why?

2   Draw a strip cartoon of what an ice cube would look like as it melts.

3   **a)** At what temperature does ice melt?
    b) At what temperature does water freeze?

4   Chocolate does not melt when you take it out of the freezer. Why?

Labels in Figure 2: thermometer, beaker, clamp stand, Bunsen burner, 100 °C, boiling water, gauze, tripod

5.4

Stop and think!

Think about this experiment. Only the hands were used to heat the beaker.

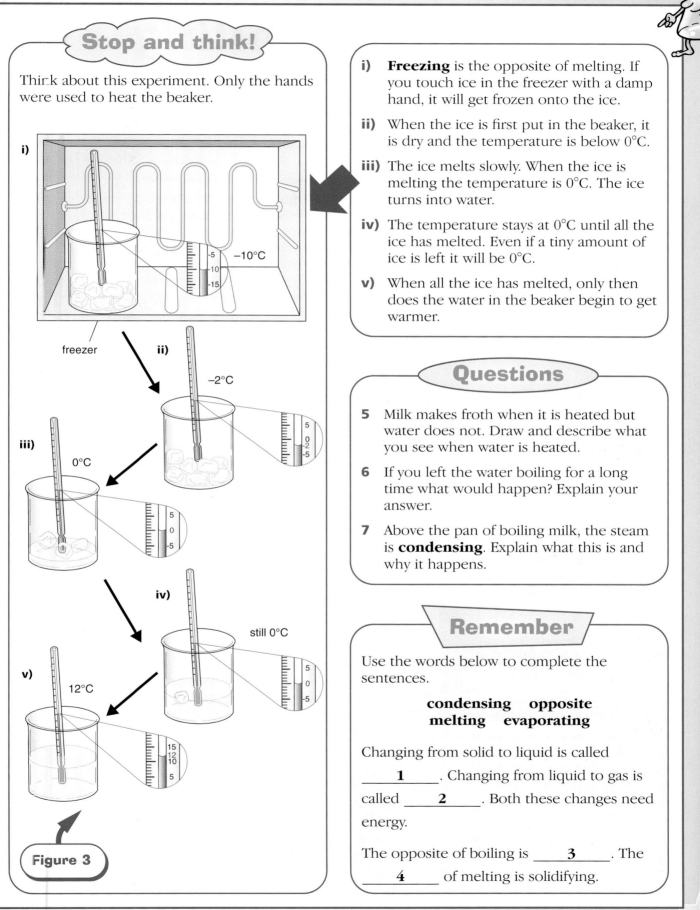

Figure 3

i) **Freezing** is the opposite of melting. If you touch ice in the freezer with a damp hand, it will get frozen onto the ice.

ii) When the ice is first put in the beaker, it is dry and the temperature is below 0°C.

iii) The ice melts slowly. When the ice is melting the temperature is 0°C. The ice turns into water.

iv) The temperature stays at 0°C until all the ice has melted. Even if a tiny amount of ice is left it will be 0°C.

v) When all the ice has melted, only then does the water in the beaker begin to get warmer.

Questions

5 Milk makes froth when it is heated but water does not. Draw and describe what you see when water is heated.

6 If you left the water boiling for a long time what would happen? Explain your answer.

7 Above the pan of boiling milk, the steam is **condensing**. Explain what this is and why it happens.

Remember

Use the words below to complete the sentences.

**condensing   opposite
melting   evaporating**

Changing from solid to liquid is called _____**1**_____. Changing from liquid to gas is called _____**2**_____. Both these changes need energy.

The opposite of boiling is _____**3**_____. The _____**4**_____ of melting is solidifying.

Gases and boiling

When a liquid boils it becomes a very large volume of gas.

Mixtures of liquids can be separated by distillation.

Solutions do not have the same boiling point as pure liquids.

Making alcool

Figure 1 Sugar cane growing.

Figure 2 An 'Alcool' station in Brazil

In Brazil they can grow lots of sugar cane. The bright tropical Sun gives lots of energy and the sugar cane stores this. The people use some of this cane to make a fuel for motor cars. The sugar is **fermented** with yeast in big tanks, like when beer and wine are made. This turns most of the sugar into a chemical called **ethanol**. Ethanol is a fuel; it burns easily. The Brazilians give it the name 'Alcool'.

When the fermentation is finished a mixture of ethanol, water and yeast is left. This is useless as a fuel until it has been distilled.

Fractional distillation is a process that can be used to separate a mixture of **liquids** because they all boil at different temperatures.

Ethanol boils at a lower temperature than water. It vaporises first when the mixture is heated. The vapour is condensed to give a fuel that is nearly pure ethanol.

At the cold end of the scale

If you cool a gas, such as steam or candle wax vapour, it turns back into a liquid.

But you can also turn a gas into a liquid just by compressing it – squeezing it into a smaller space. The particles get pushed closer and closer together until they are touching. This is how liquid air is made.

Liquid air is a very cold mixture. The different substances in liquid air can be separated by distillation because they have different boiling points. Oxygen has a boiling point of $-183°C$, argon has a boiling point of $-186°C$ and nitrogen boils at $-196°C$. Pure gases are produced by this process.

Questions

1 What is the fuel made from sugar called?

2 How is the sugar turned into this fuel?

3 What mixture needs to be separated in this process?

4 How do they get the fuel out of the mixture? Explain how the process works.

5 At what temperature does liquid oxygen boil?

6 How is it separated from nitrogen and argon?

Boiling

Liquid particles are in contact because of **air pressure** pushing down on them. Remember the 'carnival' idea of liquids. If one of the people watching in the crowd starts moving really quickly, they can escape out of the 'crowd' into the dancing procession.

Figure 3

To turn a liquid into a gas the **particles** need to move faster. They need to be moving fast enough to escape from the forces which keep them together. Energy makes them move faster.

You can see the steam rising from the surface of hot water as just a few water particles escape. As the temperature nears 100°C, all the particles are moving fast enough. Large holes appear in the liquid and the water boils.

Generally, the lighter the liquid particle, the easier it is to make it speed up. So lightweight liquid particles boil at lower temperatures, heavier liquid particles have a higher **boiling point**. But there are exceptions to this.

Figure 4 Raise the pressure and water boils at a higher temperature. In a pressure cooker water boils at 115°C. In hospitals the high temperature is used to sterilise equipment in a machine called an autoclave, seen here.

Figure 5 Lower the pressure and water boils at a lower temperature. High up a mountain water boils at 80°C, so you can't make good tea.

Questions

7 What is the difference between a liquid and a gas? Draw particle pictures to explain.

8 What does air do to stop a liquid turning into a gas?

9 What happens to the speed of movement of particles as they get hotter?

10 Explain the difference between evaporation and boiling.

11 Why does water boil at a higher temperature in a pressure cooker? Explain by writing about the speed of the particles.

Remember

Match the words to the spaces.

pressure   lower   fractional distillation fast   particles   boiling   lighter   liquids

_____**1**_____ happens when the liquid

_____**2**_____ are moving quickly. They have to

be moving _____**3**_____ enough to overcome

the push of the air _____**4**_____ on the liquid.

_____**5**_____ particles move faster, so lighter

particles have a _____**6**_____ boiling point.

Sorting _____**7**_____ by boiling point is called

_____**8**_____ .

Closer

Data for winter freeze

Antifreeze is a solution that cools the car engine but doesn't freeze in winter frosts. Without it we'd be walking every time it snowed!

Winters are getting colder. The lowest temperatures used to be −10 °C, but now −18 °C could be expected.

A car designer carried out experiments and collected results to predict how they could best protect car engines.

The results are shown in the table.

% of antifreeze in the coolant solution	Temperature the solution froze (°C)		
	First try	Second try	Third try
0	0	0	0
10	−8	−7	−8
20	−13	−14	−12
30	−18	−18	−19
40	−25	−30	−20
50	−40	−50	−30

Questions

1  What happens to the freezing temperature as you put more antifreeze in the cooling solution?
2 Why have the measurements been taken three times, rather than taken just once or twice?
3 Plot a graph to show the pattern of the results. You could use a computer application, or graph paper to do this.
4 Explain why you can be sure about the pattern shown in the results?
5 The car designer is less confident in the measurements they have taken for the 40% and 50% antifreeze solutions. Explain why.
6 What advice would the designer give about how much antifreeze to use?

Thinklinks

Draw a thinklinks map to link these terms:

**solvent   solution   solute   concentrated   dilute   saturated   temperature
distillation   chromatography**

Use a search engine on the web to learn more

Use one of these phrases for an internet search, then write 50 words that sum up what you found out.

- Fluoride in drinking water.
- Is bottled water better or worse than tap water?
- UK water supply companies.

CHAPTER 6

Force and motion

Opener Activity
Diving forces

There are forces all the way for a diver. When she stands on the diving board the force of gravity is pulling her downwards. But the diving board pushes upwards on her feet. The forces are in balance.

The diver moves clear of the diving board. There's no upwards force any more. She accelerates down until she hits the water. The water provides a force of resistance that slows the diver to a stop.

Questions

Think about three forces:

- downwards force of gravity (which is the weight of the diver)
- upwards force provided by the diving board
- upwards force provided by the water.

1 Which of the forces are acting when:

a) the diver is standing on the diving board?
b) the diver is falling towards the water?
c) the diver is going into the water?

2 Which of the forces do you think could be dangerous?

3 Why do you think the diver isn't scared to jump?

69

Speed, time and distance

Speed, time and distance are quantities that are linked together.

Figure 1 The police have to protect people from speeding drivers. They can use radar guns or cameras to measure the speed of cars.

Figure 2 The 'speedo' on the car tells the driver the speed, instant by instant.

This is the pattern that links speed, distance and time:

$$\text{Speed} = \frac{\text{Distance travelled}}{\text{Time taken}}$$

That means that speed is the same as distance divided by time.

In some areas, the speed limit is 50 kilometres per hour. If a car travels at that speed for one hour then it will travel a distance of 50 kilometres. These are the quantities involved:

speed = 50 kilometres per hour
distance = 50 kilometres
time = 1 hour

We can put the information into a table and add extra information. For example, if the car kept up the same speed for two hours it would go twice as far. We can show what happens at other speeds (see Table 1).

We can work out the speed of the sprinter in Figure 3 by dividing the distance by the time.

distance = 100 metres
time = 10 seconds
speed = ?

Speed = distance ÷ time
that's 100 metres divided by 10 seconds

Speed = 100 metres ÷ 10 seconds
100 divided by 10 is 10

So the sprinter runs at 10 metres per second.
Speed = 10 metres per second

Speed in kilometres per hour	Time in hours	Distance travelled in kilometres
40	1	40
50	1	50
120	1	120
40	2	80
50	2	100
120	2	240

Table 1

Figure 3 An Olympic sprinter

For a cheetah that travels 100 metres in 4 seconds:

distance = 100 metres
time = 4 seconds
speed = ?

To find the speed we divide the distance by the time.

Speed = distance ÷ time
that's 100 metres divided by 4 seconds
Speed = 100 metres ÷ 4 seconds
100 divided by 4 is 25
So the answer is 25 metres per second.
Speed = 25 metres per second

Figure 4 A cheetah

Questions

1 a) A car travels at a steady 60 kilometres per hour for 1 hour. How far does it go?
   b) Predict how far it can go in two hours at the same speed.

2 a) If a runner goes at a steady 6 metres per second for 1 second, how far does she go?
   b) How far will she go in
       i)   2 seconds?
       ii) 10 seconds?
       iii) 100 seconds?

3 a) Make a bar chart to show the speeds of the sprinter and the cheetah.
   b) Make another bar chart to show the different times they take to travel 100 metres.
   c) Compare the two bar charts. What are the main differences?

4 Suppose that you walk 4 metres in 2 seconds. Copy and complete the following to work out what your speed would be:

speed = distance ÷ time
that's 4 metres divided by 2 seconds

speed = _____ metres ÷ _____ seconds
4 divided by 2 is 2

so speed is _____ metres per second.

Remember

Match the words below to the spaces.

**distance   hour   time   metres
kilometres   seconds**

A speed limit in a town might be 50 ____1____ per hour. On a motorway the speed limit might be 120 kilometres per ____2____. Sometimes it is better to measure speed in metres per second. Then distance is measured in ____3____ and time is measured in ____4____.

We can work out speed in the same way for different moving things. We can write:

speed = ____5____ ÷ ____6____

Different kinds of force

There are different kinds of force. We can measure a force by seeing how much it stretches a spring. The force of gravity acting on an object is called its weight.

Moons and magnets

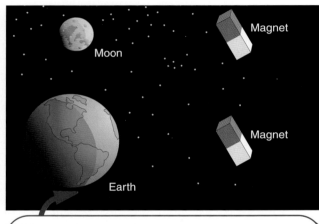

Figure 1 Forces of gravity and magnetism can act without touching.

The force of **gravity** is a force that attracts. It acts everywhere on the Earth. It also acts above the Earth. You can still feel it if you are in a plane or the basket of a hot-air balloon.

The Moon has its own pull of gravity. The Moon and the Earth are in a never-ending dance, held together by their combined gravity.

You don't have to be as big as the Moon or the Earth to feel the force of gravity. We all feel it, and it keeps us trapped on the surface of the Earth. The force of gravity acting on your body is called your **weight**.

Forces also act between two magnets. The magnets don't have to be touching each other. Magnets can repel each other. They can also attract each other like the Earth and the Moon do. But the force between magnets is not a force of gravity. It's a different kind of force – **magnetic force**.

Stretching and measuring

A force is needed to stretch a rubber band. You can provide the force with your fingers. Or you can get gravity to provide the force by hanging masses from the rubber band.

A spring also stretches. We can use the stretch of a spring to measure force. The amount of stretch is sometimes called the **extension** of the spring. We need a spring with a hook, and a **scale** for making the measurements. The scale is marked with numbers, and there is a **unit** for measuring force, called a **newton**.

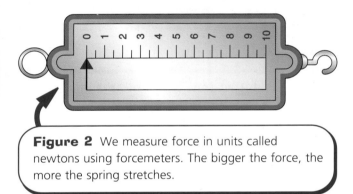

Figure 2 We measure force in units called newtons using forcemeters. The bigger the force, the more the spring stretches.

Forces of resistance

A force can make something start moving. But forces can also act against movement. When you ride a bike fast you can feel the air pushing against you. There is a force of **air resistance** acting against your movement.

As the wheels of the bike go round they have to slide round their axles. Whenever one surface slides across another there is **friction**. This produces a force that resists the movement. It can also make the surfaces hotter. Air resistance and friction forces are forces that act against motion.

Weight and mass

One newton is about the size of force that's needed to pick up an apple. We say that one newton is the weight of the apple.

The weight of an apple is not the same thing as its **mass**. Weight is the force of gravity that pulls the apple downwards. We measure it in newtons. But we measure mass in kilograms.

Figure 4 The weight of an apple is about 1 newton.

Figure 3 Isaac Newton was the first person to say that the force that acts between the Earth and the Moon is the same kind of force that holds us all on the surface of the Earth.

Remember

Fill in the spaces using the following words.

**newton   extension   gravity   scale
repel   weight   unit   mass**

Magnets can attract or _____**1**_____ each other.

The force of _____**2**_____ acts between big objects like the Earth and the Moon. It also acts on objects like apples. The force of gravity acting on an apple is called its _____**3**_____.

We can measure force by measuring the _____**4**_____ of a spring. The _____**5**_____ we use for measuring force is called a _____**6**_____, after Sir Isaac Newton. A forcemeter has a _____**7**_____ which we can read to see how big the force is. _____**8**_____ is measured in kilograms and it is not the same thing as weight.

Questions

1 Which of these words describes the force of gravity pulling you towards the Earth?

friction   speed   magnetism   weight
air resistance

2 What would life be like if the force of gravity made the Earth repel you instead of attracting you?

3 Copy and complete this table by writing 'yes' or 'no' in the spaces:

	Force of gravity	Magnetic force
Can act without touching		
Only provides forces of attraction		
Provides forces of attraction and repulsion (repelling)		

Balanced and unbalanced forces

Balanced forces can keep you going at a steady speed. Unbalanced forces can make you change speed or change direction.

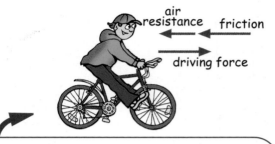

Figure 3 Easing off on the pedals – slowing down gently. If you make the driving force small then it is not big enough to balance the friction and air resistance any more. Forces acting against your movement are bigger than the driving force. The forces are **unbalanced**. You slow down.

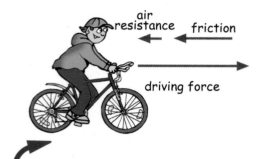

Figure 1 Starting off. We can use arrows to show the size and direction of the forces. There's friction in the moving parts of the bike. But at low speed there isn't much air resistance acting against you. If you exert a big **driving force**, you'll go faster and faster. You'll **accelerate**.

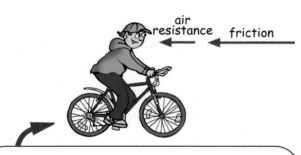

Figure 4 Braking. If you need to stop in a hurry, you can increase friction by using your brakes. Now the forces are strongly unbalanced and you slow down quickly.

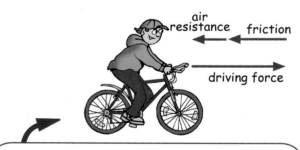

Figure 2 Cruising along. Friction and air resistance provide forces that resist movement. There is more air resistance at high speed. But if your driving force matches the resistive forces, you'll keep going at a steady speed. You don't accelerate any more. The forces are **balanced**.

Unbalanced force produces acceleration

Figure 5 The diver is **accelerating** towards the Earth. An accelerating object has a changing speed. You need an unbalanced force to accelerate. Gravity is providing this force.

force of gravity

Balanced forces mean no acceleration

upward force provided by the weightlifter

the forces acting on the 'weights'

force of gravity acting on the 'weights'

Figure 6 Everything accelerates towards the Earth unless there is an upwards force to balance the weight. Weight is another name for the force of gravity. The weightlifter has to struggle to provide an upwards force that's big enough.
The 'weights' get their name from the force that's pulling them downwards.

Remember

Use the following words to complete the sentences.

**air balanced friction accelerate
unbalanced driving gravity weight**

When you are moving there are forces acting against your movement. These are ____1____ and ____2____ resistance. You will slow down and stop unless you exert a ____3____ force. When the forces are ____4____ you will keep going at a steady speed. When the forces are ____5____ your speed will change. For example, if the driving force is bigger than the resistive forces then you will ____6____.

There is a force of attraction between the Earth and other objects. It is called the force of ____7____. The force of gravity acting on an object is called the ____8____ of the object.

Questions

1 a) On a bike, what happens to your speed when the forces acting on you are balanced?

   b) What happens when the driving force is bigger than the resistive forces?

2 Do a simple drawing of a cyclist who is starting off and accelerating. Add arrows to show

   a) force of friction

   b) force of air resistance

   c) driving force.

3 The diver accelerates to the Earth. The weightlifter's weights do not. What makes the difference?

4 a) Sort these situations into 'balanced force' and 'unbalanced force'.

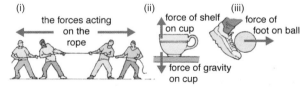

(i) the forces acting on the rope

(ii) force of shelf on cup / force of gravity on cup

(iii) force of foot on ball

   b) Which of the objects are changing speed?

5 These are situations with balanced forces. Copy and add arrows to show the balancing force.

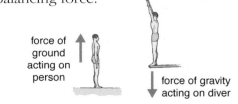

force of ground acting on person

force of gravity acting on diver

Wheelchair speed

When everyday objects move, there are forces that resist their movement. To keep going at a steady speed there must be another force to balance the forces that resist.

Figure 1 This is Heinz Frei finishing the London marathon for parathletes. He's just travelled 42 kilometres in about 2 hours. We can work out his **average speed**:
Heinz's speed = distance travelled ÷ time.
That's 42 kilometres divided by 2 hours
Heinz's speed = 42 kilometres ÷ 2 hours
42 divided by 2 is 21
So his average speed was 21 kilometres per hour.

Forces

Most of the way around the course, Heinz has to work hard to keep up a steady speed. He has to keep pushing. If he didn't, he'd soon stop. Forces of **air resistance** and **friction** are acting against his movement all the time.

Figure 4 Heinz has to keep on pushing to overcome the forces that have slowing effects. If Heinz's force matches these forces, he won't slow down. The forces will be balanced. He'll keep going at a steady speed. Heinz's forward force could be called a **driving force**.

force of air resistance

Figure 2 Forces of air resistance are sometimes called **drag** forces. Drag has a slowing down effect.

force of friction

Figure 3 When surfaces touch each other it can be hard for them to slide. It's hard for the wheel to slide against the axle that's holding it – that's friction. Forces of friction have slowing down effects.

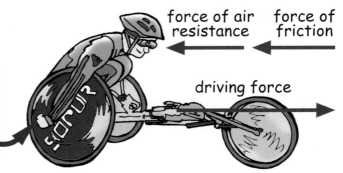

force of air resistance   force of friction

driving force

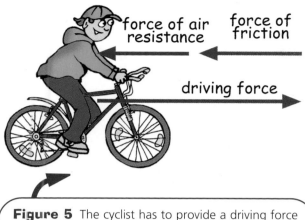

Figure 5 The cyclist has to provide a driving force to go at steady speed. Forces of air resistance and friction act against his motion. He can feel the force of air resistance. It feels like wind blowing in his face. The faster he goes, the bigger the air resistance.

Remember

Unscramble the words to complete the paragraph.

You can work out speed by dividing distance by <u>EMIT</u>. An object like a parathlete, a cyclist or a bus has to overcome forces of friction and air <u>NICER SEATS</u> to keep a steady speed. Force of air resistance can also be called <u>GARD</u> force. The parathlete, the cyclist and the bus have to provide a <u>V RIDING</u> force to make sure that all the forces are in balance.

Questions

1   A runner in a marathon race covers 42 kilometres in 3 hours. Copy this and fill in the gaps:

Runner's speed = _____ travelled ÷ time taken

that's 42 kilometres divided by _____ hours

Runner's speed = _____ kilometres ÷ _____ hours

_____ divided by 3 is 14

So the runner's average speed is _____ kilometres per hour.

2   As the cyclist speeds up, she feels more wind resistance. Air is made of particles. Draw a particle picture to show why the resistance is greater as she goes faster.

3   Copy and complete these sketches of Heinz when he is going **a)** slowly and **b)** fast. Add arrows to show the driving force Heinz must exert to balance the forces that resist his movement.

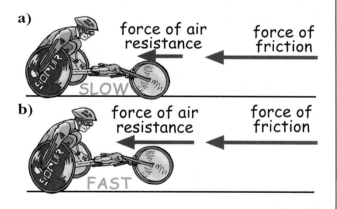

4   If you ride in a car and travel 42 kilometres in 1 hour, what is your average speed?

6.5

Floating and swimming in water

A floating object is pulled down by a force of gravity that is balanced by an upwards force provided by the water. Water exerts stronger drag forces than air does.

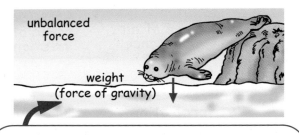

Figure 1 A common seal.

A fully grown seal is a large animal. It would be hard to pick one up even if you could get close enough. A seal has a lot of weight.

Figure 2 Weight is a downwards force. It makes objects accelerate downwards when there is no upwards force to balance it. That's what happens to a seal that dives off a rock or an iceberg.

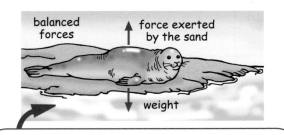

Figure 3 When a seal is resting on a sandy beach the sand exerts an upwards force.

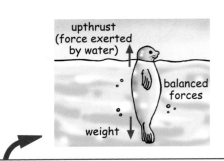

Figure 4 A seal can rest in water as well. When a seal is in water, the water provides an upwards force to balance its weight. This force exerted by the water is called **upthrust**. When upthrust balances weight, the motion of an object doesn't change.

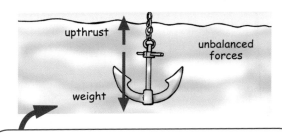

Figure 5 If upthrust is smaller than weight, the object accelerates downwards. An anchor of a boat has a lot of weight and water can't provide enough upthrust to balance it. An anchor accelerates downwards when it's dropped underwater.

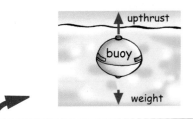

Figure 6 A buoy is meant to float. If you took one under water it would experience a big upthrust and it would accelerate back to the surface as soon as you let go of it.

Dolphin speed

Table 1 Dolphins can swim at speeds of up to 20 metres per second. We can put data about dolphin speed into a table.

Speed in metres per second	20	20	20	20	20	20	20
Time in seconds	1	2	3	4	10	60 (1 minute)	300 (5 minutes)
Distance in metres	20	40		80		1200	

Figure 6 Dolphin speed

Question

1 Copy the dolphin speed table and fill in the gaps.

Dolphin force

A dolphin uses its flippers and its strong tail to push water backwards. The backwards push on the water creates a forward push on the dolphin. The forward push is the **thrust**.

Water exerts big **drag** forces. Drag is the name of the force of resistance acting on anything that moves through air or water. Dolphins need strong muscular forces to create enough thrust to balance the drag.

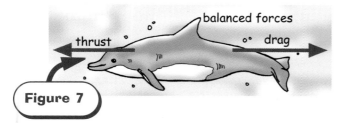

Figure 7

Questions

2 a) Plot a graph of speed against time for a dolphin swimming at 20 metres per second. Put 'time in seconds' on the horizontal axis.
b) Plot a graph of distance against time for the dolphin.

3 Draw sketches of:
a) a stone that's been dropped into water.
b) a beach ball that's been held under water and then let go.
c) a beach ball floating on water.

Add arrows to show the weight (downwards force) acting on each object. Add arrows to show upthrust (upwards force) acting on each object. Use different lengths of arrow to show the different sizes of the upwards and downwards forces.

Remember

Match the words to the spaces.

thrust   drag   balanced   upthrust

Any body, such as a seal, an anchor or a buoy, will accelerate upwards or downwards unless the upwards and downwards forces acting on it are _____**1**_____. An upwards force in water is called _____**2**_____.

A swimming dolphin experiences resistive forces of _____**3**_____. It can balance the force of drag by working to create a forwards force of _____**4**_____.

Closer

Dangerous forces, safe forces

Acceleration is what happens whenever motion changes. The change could involve starting off or speeding up, slowing down or stopping, or even just changing direction.

In an accident, motion changes rapidly. There is a lot of acceleration. And big acceleration needs big force. The trouble is that human bodies are squidgy, soft and fragile. They are not as good as dummies, like this, at standing up to large forces. Car accidents can kill.

At a theme park, forces are very carefully planned to thrill and not to kill.

Activity

1 In which of the pictures, if any, can you see:

   a) balanced forces

   b) downwards acceleration

   c) high resistive force

   d) change in motion involving change in direction

   e) upthrust.

2 Why are the forces at a theme park safe but forces in a car accident dangerous?

CHAPTER 7

Variation and classification

Opener Activity
Triassic terrors

Although we have fossilised bones from dinosaurs and some very rare impressions of dinosaur skin in rock, we don't know what colour the dinosaurs were. What colour do you think they were? Are the children in the cartoon right or wrong, or could they be partly right?

I think that dinosaurs must have been shades of brown and green so that they were camouflaged in the jungle.

I think they were brightly coloured, maybe purple, yellow and red so that they could attract mates.

I think that the males were brightly coloured and the females were dull, like peacocks.

Questions

1 Impressions of dinosaur skin show that they had skin like a reptile. What colour skin can reptiles have? Make a list of some reptiles you know about and what colour their skin is.

2 Some dinosaurs were very large. What colour skin do our largest land animals have?

3 Birds are the modern descendents of dinosaurs and they come in all sorts of colours. Does this fact help us decide what colour skin the dinosaurs had? Explain your answer.

4 Prepare a statement about your thoughts on the colours of dinosaurs. Include your ideas about the possible skin colours of the following types of prehistoric animals:

a) Large plant-eating dinosaur.
b) Small (dog sized) meat-eating dinosaurs.
c) Large meat-eating dinosaurs (like T. rex).
d) Very small (chicken sized) scavenging dinosaurs.
e) Flying pterosaurs and pterydactyls.

Variation

All people are different. These differences can be due to the environment or the genes we inherit from our parents.

Look at the person sitting next to you. Do they look the same or are they different from you? They may be of a different sex, they may have different coloured eyes or hair, or they may be taller, shorter, bigger or smaller. They also have lots of things that are the same as you: two eyes, two ears, two arms and two legs.

When scientists look at the differences between living organisms, they are studying the **variation** between them. Some variations between living things are easy to see – for example a mouse has four legs and so does an elephant, but it is easy to spot the difference! It is also easy to see why the mouse and elephant have legs of different shapes. Other variations will be more difficult to see, such as a person's blood group.

Figure 1

Continuous and discontinuous variation

Scientists look at two different types of variation in living things – **continuous variation** and **discontinuous variation**.

In discontinuous variation, the variation must be one thing or another. For example, eyes are generally either blue or green or brown; natural hair colour is usually blond or brown or black or auburn. In continuous variation, things can have any value in a **range** of values. For example, a person's height might be anywhere between, say, 30 cm when they are born to about 2 m as an adult (quite tall!). People are *not* either 1 m or 1.5 m or 2 m tall!

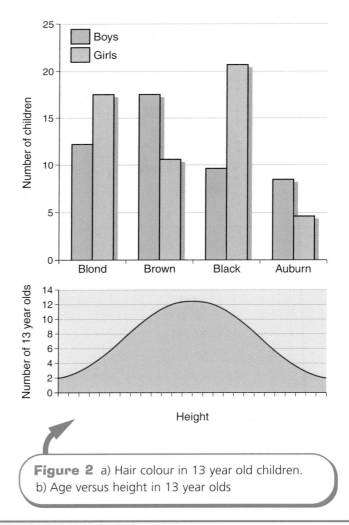

Figure 2 a) Hair colour in 13 year old children.
b) Age versus height in 13 year olds

Reasons for variation

Variation in living things has different causes. Where we live and how we are brought up can cause variation, even between identical twins. If one twin overeats and happens to live in a hot country, they would end up bigger and heavier than their twin. They may have a darker skin colour because they sunbathe a lot. This sort of variation is called **environmental variation**. In plants, environmental variation can affect how well the plants grow. There are four very important things that can affect how well a plant grows:

1 light
2 water
3 temperature
4 type of soil.

Figure 3 The family resemblance between the four member of The Corrs is obvious.

If you look at your natural parents or the photograph in Figure 3, you will see that there are some characteristics or features that run in families, for example the shape of the nose, the type of hair and hair colour. This means that you will look like your natural parents or brother or sister. These are characteristics that we inherit from our parents through their **genes**. This variation is known as **inherited variation**.

1 Do a survey of your fellow class members and produce two charts like the ones in Figure 2.

2 Are your charts similar to or different from the ones in the diagram? In what ways are they similar and in what ways are they different?

3 If you could survey all the pupils in year 7, do you think your charts would be even more similar to the charts here? If not why not?

4 If your height survey was done on all of the teachers in your school, how might the shape of the chart change?

5 Many people change the colour of their hair. Sketch how this would affect your graph if there was a craze for bleached hair.

6 Would your graph from Question 5 be a scientific 'fair test'? Explain your answer.

7 Classify these variables as continuous or discontinuous variation.

  • Finger length

  • Foot length

  • Shoe size

  • Eye colour

  • Arm span

8 Explain the difference between 'shoe size' and 'foot length'.

Remember

All species are different from each other, but within a certain species (like human beings) all the individuals are different as well.

There is discontinuous variation like hair colour and continuous variation such as height.

What causes variation?

Variation can be caused by differences in environment or inherited characteristics.

No two people are alike, unless they are identical twins. Even then there can be differences. Look at the identical twins in Figure 1. They look the same but one of them is slightly fatter and taller. Some of their features or characteristics are identical, such as their eye colour, hair colour, the shape of the nose and mouth. Other features are not, such as the height and their weight. In the last spread we found out about environmental variation. Let's look a little further into inherited and environmental variation.

Figure 1 Geoff and James are genetically identical twins, but Geoff is smaller than James due to environmental factors.

Question

1 We all inherit some characteristics from our mother and father. Look at the characteristics in boxes below and decide which ones can be inherited, which ones can be environmental and which ones could be both inherited and environmental. Make a table in your exercise book and record your decisions.

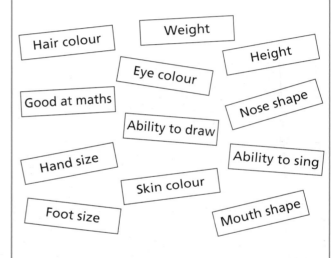

Hair colour   Weight   Height   Eye colour   Good at maths   Nose shape   Ability to draw   Hand size   Ability to sing   Skin colour   Foot size   Mouth shape

For all those characteristics you placed in both the inherited column and the environmental column explain how the characteristic could be affected by both.

Some people do not like some of the features that they inherit from their parents. They alter them by having plastic surgery. Would this stop their children inheriting the same features? To answer this question we can look at what we do to some of our animals. Dogs often have their tails cut off or docked, like the one in Figure 2. Many people believe that it is not necessary to dock tails. We cause this change to a dog's characteristics and we have been doing it for hundreds of years. Are dogs more likely to be born now without tails? The answer is no, otherwise we would not have to continue docking their tails!

If you look at the two photos in Figure 3 you will see that although the plants are the same, the colour of the flower is not. Pink and white hydrangeas grow in soil that is chalky (alkaline), blue hydrangeas grow in soil that is acid.

Figure 2 Although this dog has had its tail docked, it doesn't mean its puppies will be born with docked tails.

Plants and animals can also have inherited and/ or environmental variation. Trees growing in windy areas tend to be thinner, mammals living in colder areas tend to have thicker coats, and flowers grown in different types of soil may have the colour of the flower determined by the type of soil.

Questions

2 Which of the following features do you think can be affected by the environment or the way in which someone is brought up?

Hair colour, weight, skin colour, length of the index finger.

3 A man with ears that stuck out had them pinned back using plastic surgery. He was convinced that this would stop any of his children having the same type of ears. Say if you think he is right or wrong and why.

4 Explain why identical twins separated at birth may not be identical if they meet up 30 years later. What may be the same about them and what might be different?

5 'If identical twin men married identical twin women, their children would not be identical to each other, but they could look similar.' Explain why this statement is true.

Figure 3 The colour of the hydrangea flower depends on the type of soil.

Charles Darwin

Charles Darwin was born in England in 1809. He was the son of a doctor. When he was about your age he started collecting things, and he learnt to observe carefully.

In 1831 he volunteered to sail on a survey ship, the *HMS Beagle*, which was travelling to South America. It was a scientific survey to gather animal and fossil specimens. The voyage lasted five years. For Charles Darwin it was a unique adventure and the starting point of his life as a great scientist.

When the ship found landfall, Darwin went and searched for interesting animals and plants. He filled many notebooks with thousands of observations. He made studies of living things that had not been seen elsewhere and found many unusual rocks and minerals.

On the voyage, the Galapagos Islands were of particular interest. He found some very strange animals there. There were huge lizards called iguanas, and Darwin observed no less than fourteen different varieties of finch, each with a different shape of beak. Darwin realised that the beaks of the birds had adapted to eating a certain type of food. For example, the finch species that ate insects had a different shaped beak from those that ate

seeds. Darwin was such a good scientist because he noticed details like this. He closely observed things, then asked himself questions like:

- Why are some animals so similar and yet they live on islands far away from each other?
- Why are some animals in the same species slightly different from each other?
- What causes the differences?

The theory of why animals change

There was already a theory about why animals gradually change over the years. A scientist called Lamarck had proposed that some 'vital force' made animals change. He believed that giraffes have long necks because they have to stretch upwards to reach the leaves on the high trees. Lamarck said that the stretched neck of the giraffe would be passed on to its children and that this explained the gradual lengthening of the neck of the giraffe over many years.

Darwin sent samples back to Britain so that he could study them in more detail when he returned. After many years of study, he finally worked out how one kind of living thing could change slowly into another kind over a long period of time – a process called evolution. Darwin called his idea the theory of natural selection. He said that evolution happens because of the slight variation between organisms of the same species. For example, giraffes have offspring that are all slightly different. The ones with longer necks are more likely to survive than those with shorter necks

Figure 1 Charles Darwin

because they can reach higher into the trees to eat the leaves. Because of this, it is the longer-necked giraffes which survive long enough to have children, so they will pass on their long neck to the next generation. Over the years, this lead to a gradual increase in the length of giraffes' necks.

Darwin wrote a famous book called *On the Origin of Species by Means of Natural Selection* to explain his ideas. It was a bestseller in 1859. Another famous scientist called Alfred Russel Wallace contributed nearly as much as Darwin to the development of the theory of evolution, but he is often forgotten in the shadow of the more famous man. Some of the ideas of Darwin and Wallace still cause arguments today, particularly in the USA where 'creationism' – the idea that God created the Earth as it is today – is sometimes given equal weight.

Questions

1 What was the name of the ship Darwin sailed on?

2 How long was the voyage?

3 What was the purpose of the voyage?

4 How old was Darwin when he left?

5 How old was he when he published his famous book?

6 What was the book called?

7 Explain in your own words Lamarck's theory of why animals change. Give a different example to the one in the passage.

8 Explain in your own words Darwin's theory of why animals change.

9 What questions did Darwin ask himself about wildlife he observed?

10 What is creationism?

Scientists

Professor Steve Jones, Geneticist

Charles Darwin studied worms and barnacles for many years. Professor Steve Jones, the geneticist, studies snails. He was born in 1944 in Wales and for many years did not think of a career as a scientist. Although both his parents were scientists – his mother was a bacteriologist and his father a chemist who helped to invent the household cleaner 'Cif' (then called 'Jif') – he claims that he was much better at English in school and science was not his best subject. His interest in science started when he took up birdwatching and, after finishing school he went to the University of Edinburgh where he was awarded a science degree and then a doctorate. He is currently Professor of Genetics at University College London (UCL) and writes books on evolution and makes television programmes that popularise science.

Some people call Professor Jones the Darwin of the 21st Century.

A select group

Scientists can breed plants and animals with particular characteristics by a process called selective breeding.

Selective breeding

Wheat is a very important crop. All over the world it provides food for millions. The wheat that we grow today, however, is very different to the wheat grown by people thousands of years ago. Originally wheat was quite a tall plant with few grains. Today, the wheat that grows in the fields is much shorter and contains a larger number of grains. This is an example of **selective breeding**. Farmers have been selectively breeding plants and animals for thousands of years. As a result of this we have cows that produce more milk, sheep that have longer woollen fleeces, bigger tomatoes, fatter turkeys, faster race-horses and more compact cabbages.

Selective breeding is not just about food production. Some people selectively breed living things to try and improve on them or to ensure that the breeds of cat or dog, for example, stay pure.

Racehorses are selectively bred. People who are involved in that sport keep very accurate records. They record how many races the father and mother of a young horse had won in their time. This is a good indicator – but does not guarantee success!

By taking a fast male race-horse and a mare that is also a good race-horse, breeders can mate them with each other in the hope of producing a champion horse. Dog breeders do the same; by mating dogs that have the perfect features for their breed, they hope to produce a dog that can win the best of breed category at Crufts annual dog show. In plants, breeders might use a plant that is resistant to disease to produce other varieties that are resistant to disease.

Figure 1 The Jacob sheep (left) is an ancient breed of sheep. Farmers used selective breeding on species similar to this to produce modern sheep species like those above.

What's new?

Rose growers are always trying to breed new varieties of roses. They select roses that have particular characteristics, such as smell, size, number of flowers or colour. They take the pollen from one rose, perhaps with a nice perfume, and place it on another rose with another feature such as large red flowers. By doing this they hope to produce a new variety of rose that has large red flowers and a nice perfume. Rose growers often name their new varieties of roses after famous people that they admire.

Figure 2 The Picasso rose (top) and the Queen Mother rose (bottom) were bred by selecting features of other roses and combining them.

Questions

1 What advantage is there in breeding shorter varieties of wheat? (*Hint:* think about what could happen in different types of weather!)

2 Selective breeding could mean that some varieties of plants and animals may become extinct. If this happens we will lose all of their characteristics, good and bad. Why do you think it is important to preserve rare plants and animals?

3 What are the characteristics you would selectively breed into
  a) a domestic dog?
  b) a sheep for wool?
  c) a pig for meat?
  d) an apple tree?
  e) a strawberry plant?

4 All our cereal crops, like wheat, oats and barley, have been selectively bred from wild grasses. Explain how you think it was done.

Remember

Complete the following passage by filling in the spaces with the words in the list below.

**flower   pollen   characteristics
varieties   select   smell   colour**

For many thousands of years, farmers and breeders have been breeding new ____**1**____ of crops and animals. They ____**2**____ plants and animals that show ____**3**____ that they want and breed them with other plants and animals that have other useful characteristics. By this method new varieties are produced. Rose growers can use the ____**4**____ from one rose to fertilise another rose. This way they can produce a new variety that has some of the features of one plant and some of the other, such as ____**5**____, ____**6**____ and type of ____**7**____.

Belonging together

Scientists identify living organisms by using similarities and differences or variations in living things to place them into groups.

Look about you at the living world. Obviously some things can be grouped together, like lions and tigers, oak trees and apple trees. But for others, like a scorpion and a house spider, it is not obvious that they come from the same family.

Classification

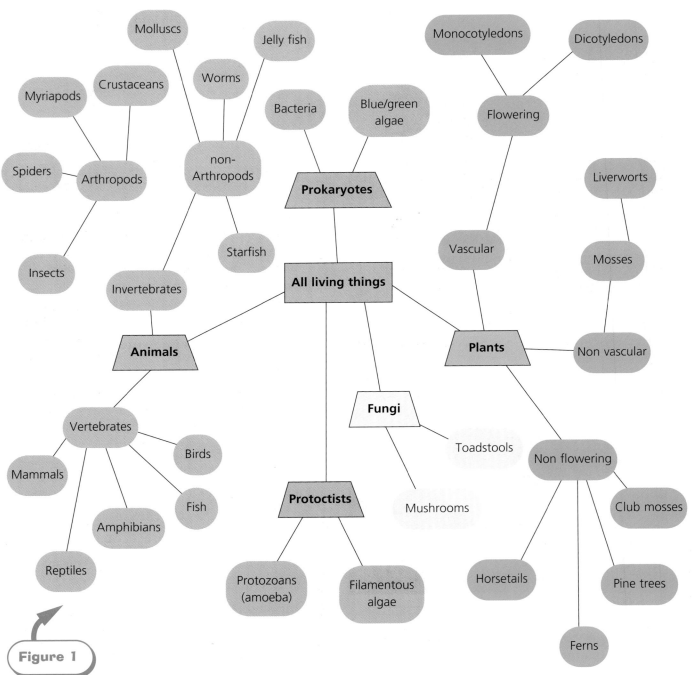

Figure 1

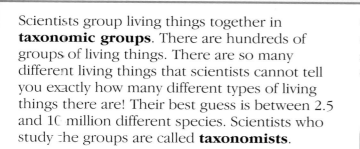

Scientists group living things together in **taxonomic groups**. There are hundreds of groups of living things. There are so many different living things that scientists cannot tell you exactly how many different types of living things there are! Their best guess is between 2.5 and 10 million different species. Scientists who study the groups are called **taxonomists**.

Whale evolution

Whales belong to a group known as *cetaceans* (pronounced see-tay-tions) which also includes dolphins and porpoises.

About 55 million years ago the ancestors of whales lived on land.

The oldest relative of whales was probably a wolf-like creature with a long snout and teeth suited to eating plants and animals.

The first partially aquatic animal, *pakicetus*, is known from a skull found in Pakistan, hence its name (the whale from Pakistan).

The first truly aquatic ancestor is an animal whose skeleton showed that its limbs were designed to work in water, although it could also walk on land. It is called *ambulocetus* (ambulo- means walking, so this translates to the walking whale).

40 million years ago the whales lived only in water. Their vertebrae (bones in the spine) had large muscles attached to them to move their tail to swim in the water. Their bodies were long and slender to help them move through the water.

Over the next 40 million years two groups of cetaceans evolved, some that were filter feeders and others that retained their teeth like dolphins and killer whales.

Questions

1 Give a short description of what a taxonomist studies.

2 Charles says 'A bird has wings and a bat has wings, therefore a bat is a bird!' Laura disagrees. She says that bats are mammals. To decide who is correct, answer the following questions.
   a) What are the main differences between bats and birds?
   b) What does a bat have that would make it similar to humans? (Humans are mammals.)

3 Put the following plants and animals into their correct taxonomic group:
   bee, garden spider, rose, rabbit, pigeon, goldfish, pine tree, crab, earthworm, carnation.

4 Explain why a domestic cat and an African lion can be put in the same taxonomic group, even though they are so different in size.

5 The tarantula, the crab, the stag beetle, the scorpion, the lobster and the ladybird are all arthropods. Valdet, says 'No way can these all be the same group. They're too different.'

   What evidence can you think of about these animals that would persuade Valdet that he is wrong?

Remember

In your exercise book draw a branching key to all the groups of living things in Figure 1. The first two levels have been done for you.

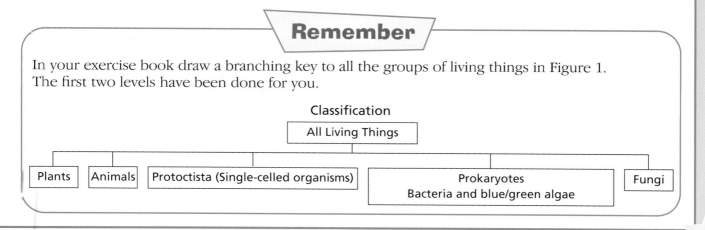

Clones

Clones are exact copies of another individual. Scientists have found ways of artificially cloning plants and animals.

Figure 1 Dolly the sheep – the first cloned mammal

The first known clone of a mammal was Dolly the sheep. Dolly was created at the Roslyn Institute in Edinburgh in 1996 by taking an egg from a ewe, removing the nucleus and injecting a new nucleus from a cell of a full grown sheep.

The egg then developed into an exact copy of the sheep from which the nucleus was taken.

Dolly died in February 2003 from lung disease.

A clone is an exact copy of another adult. Clones can occur naturally in the form of identical twins. Creating artificial clones is different. So far it has been very difficult to create full grown clones of animals, but clones of plants are very easy to make and occur everywhere. Plants can be cloned in a number of ways and some do it naturally!

Gardeners make clones when they take cuttings from plants and grow new plants from them. Strawberries have runners that grow away from the main plant and produce small plants on the end of the runners. These can take root and a new plant will grow, identical to the parent plant.

Cloning: right or wrong?

Scientists have said that it is possible to produce human clones. They also believe that it will be possible to grow human organs that can then be used as 'back-up' organs for people in case their main organs are damaged or diseased. Read the two newspaper articles reproduced opposite and decide whether or not you think that cloning of humans should be allowed.

Step 1: Take a cell from the sheep you want to clone (the donor) and grow it in a Petri dish with chemicals that stop the nucleus from working.

Step 2: Take an egg cell from a female sheep and take out the nucleus.

Step 3: Join the adult cell with the empty egg cell using an electric spark. The nucleus starts working again.

Step 4: The cell begins to grow and divide.

Step 5: The cells are transferred to the mother's womb to grow and develop as normal.

Step 6: Lambs are produced that are identical to the donor sheep.

Figure 2 How dolly was cloned

Cloning Robin Hood's tree

Scientists have produced hundreds of tiny clones of the Major Oak in Sherwood Forest and hope to grow an exact copy of Robin Hood's favourite tree.

The famous oak is said to mark the site where Robin Hood and his Merry Men set up camp. It is at least 500 years old, making it one of Britain's oldest living trees. It stands about 80 feet high, with a 36 ft circumference and a span of 240 ft.

Researchers at a small Leicestershire-based company, Micropropagation Services, are growing miniature versions of the tree in racks of glass honey jars.

The work is being carried out with help from the local council, which has allowed the scientists to remove small branches from the tree close to its main trunk.

These then bud and are grown in a culture; the shoots sprout clusters of miniature buds, each genetically identical to the next, and to the Major Oak itself. Each cluster can then be divided many times over.

The cloned trees, although genetically identical, will differ in appearance according to the climate and environment in which they grow.

The Major Oak is thought to be suffering from vandalism, old age and the attentions of millions of visitors. It may survive for several hundred years but the company intends to plant one of its clones next to it. The growing conditions of this tiny clone should match many of those of the original tree. 'Given 500 years and similar conditions they will look more or less the same,' Dr Neal Wright, managing director of the Leicestershire company, said.

At the moment only about five of every 100 buds survives, which makes the trees fairly expensive to produce at about £100 each.

Cloning human embryo

An American scientist has cloned a human embryo by splitting it in a test tube to create identical twins or triplets, in what is believed to be the first reported such experiment.

Dr Jerry Hall of George Washington University Medical Center, Washington DC, was attempting to find a way of creating extra embryos for couples undergoing infertility treatment.

The work raises important ethical questions.

Embryos can be frozen for many years and it would, in theory, be possible for identical people – twins or triplets – to be born years apart to the same woman or to others implanted with the cloned embryos. American ethicists have also raised the possibility of parents keeping a 'back-up' embryo in case their child died or needed an organ donation.

British scientists said yesterday that cloned embryos from a normal human embryo were unlikely to live.

Dr Marilyn Monk, of the Molecular Embryology Unit at the Institute of Child Health, London, said that even with perfect embryos, cloning was not feasible. If cells were 'split off' from a human embryo there would not be enough cells to allow the normal development of the embryo. Cows can be cloned because there are hundreds of cells present at an early stage.

Dr Monk said 'growing on' a few cloned embryos was far removed from producing a foetus. 'It would not work and I cannot see any point in doing it anyway; trying to justify it on the grounds that it would produce more embryos for infertility treatments is very poor and counter-productive, because they would be defective embryos.'

Cells are sometimes removed from an embryo for the purpose of genetic diagnosis and this work is being pursued at the Hammersmith Hospital in west London. However, any attempt at cloning embryos is illegal in Britain.

Remember

Prepare your own newspaper article giving your reasons either for or against cloning.

Closer

Bulldogs got their name from fighting bulls, badgers, bears and other dogs for sport, hundreds of years ago. Dog breeders have set ideas about what the perfect bulldog looks like. They have to be of a medium size with a smooth coat, heavy, low-swung body, massive head, wide shoulders and sturdy limbs. To achieve this a lot of inbreeding (breeding between closely related animals) takes place. Some vets claim that this inbreeding damages the DNA. They claim that modern bulldogs can't run, often have difficulties breathing and are unable to give birth naturally.

Most bulldogs have to be born by caesarean section (cutting open the womb) because their heads are too big to pass through the female's birth canal.

Vet Emma Milne wants the inbreeding of bulldogs stopped.

Bulldog breeding ban urged

Emma Milne, a Vet, describes the dogs as 'mutated freaks'. 'Modern bulldogs can't run, they can't breathe, they can't give birth. They have enormous problems with too much soft tissue in their mouth and it adds up to a dog that is struggling for air all its life.'

Champion bulldogs are worth up to £50,000. Males and females with the flattest faces, biggest shoulders and smallest hips are mated to produce the purest possible offspring.

Many countries have already signed up to the European Convention for the Protection of Pet Animals but British breeders fear it could change the entire look of a breed.

'What they want is some sort of Euro-dog,' say bulldog breeders.

The Kennel Club stresses the importance of health among show animals.

'There's now a statement in the breed standard that says the bulldog should not show respiratory distress,' explained a spokesman.

Questions

1   What does Emma Milne mean when she calls the dogs 'mutated freaks'?

2   Why does a modern bulldog struggle for air? What does the extra soft tissue do to prevent the dog from getting a good supply of air?

3   What does the term 'respiratory distress' mean?

4   What is preventing bulldogs with big heads from being born naturally?

5   What arguments would you use to either support the ban or carry on breeding bulldogs? Write a short statement that sets out your arguments and views on the subject.

CHAPTER 8

Acids, alkalis and salts

Sometimes the worst can happen

Every day we take risks and face hazards. 'Common sense' tells us what to do.

Lots of science activities contain hazards. To work out how risky it is to carry out an experiment you have to look carefully at what the **hazards** are.

Then you have to estimate the **chance** of something happening because of the hazard.

Identified hazards + Estimated chance = assessment of risk

Then you need to decide what safety measures to take. This will reduce the chances of something bad happening.

Questions

1   Carry out risk assessments like those in the table, for these activities. Decide what safety measures to take.
  a) Making a cup of coffee.
  b) Lighting a barbeque.
  c) Filling a petrol tank on a motorbike.
  d) Using bleach to clean the kitchen floor.
  e) Two experiments you have done in class.

Event	Hazard identification	Chance of problem happening	Risk assessment	Safety measures
Crossing motorway on foot	Fast cars, wide road, drivers don't expect you there	High probability	Very high risk – not an acceptable way to cross	Just don't cross motorway on foot
Crossing motorway by footbridge	Gust of wind strong enough to blow you off	Very low probability	Low risk – acceptable method to cross.	Watch out for gusts of wind or big cracks

Chemical opposites

Acids and alkalis are chemical opposites. Acids and alkalis are two different families of chemical substances. Families of chemicals have similar reactions.

All acids react in a similar way. One property that all acids have in common is that they change the colour of some chemicals. These chemicals are called **indicators**. **Litmus** is a coloured dye that comes from plants. When litmus is in pure water (neutral) it is purple. Acids change litmus to a **red** colour and alkalis make litmus **blue**. Neutral substances do not change the colour of litmus.

Beverley looked up the word 'acid' in a dictionary. It mentioned sour tasting. Beverley got lots of different substances from the kitchen and tested them with litmus paper. Her results are shown in Table 1.

Figure 1 Beverley testing for acids and alkalis

Substance tested	Colour with red litmus paper	Colour with blue litmus paper
lemon juice	did not change	red
salt	did not change	did not change
sour cream	did not change	red
soap	blue	did not change
grapefruit drink	did not change	red
cola drink	did not change	red
baking soda	blue	did not change
bottled water	did not change	did not change
tomato sauce	did not change	red
yoghurt	did not change	red

Table 1 Beverley's results

A thinking model

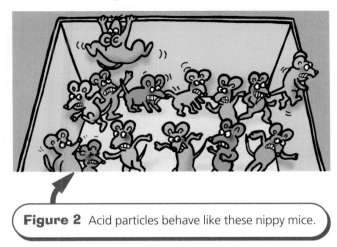

Figure 2 Acid particles behave like these nippy mice.

Acid particles are a little bit like mice. They are little nippy particles that move about 'biting' other particles and making them change. Like mice, a few acid particles are not a problem – they can even be quite useful and nice. But when there are lots and lots they become dangerous and begin to bite everything in sight. Imagine being in a box with hundreds of hungry mice!

Questions

1   Make a list of the substances that turn blue litmus to red.

2   Put a tick next to them if these substances keep red litmus red.

3   Put the heading 'acids' at the top of this list.

4   Make a list of the substances that turn red litmus to blue.

5   What heading will you put at the top of this list?

6   Make a list of the two substances which are left. Put 'neutral' as your heading.

7   Why did Beverley find more acids than alkalis in her kitchen?

8   Write down the names of other sour-tasting substances.

9   Predict if they will be acid or alkaline.

Using acids

● Metal cleaner: Acid particles change the dull oxide layer on metals so it will wash off easily.

● Vitamin C: This is added to food so that its acid particles gobble up the oxygen particles that make food go off.

● Aspirin: Acid in aspirin attacks harmful particles in our blood.

Using alkalis

Figure 3 These substances all contain alkalis.

Alkalis have different active particles in them. They are often used to destroy grease. Oven cleaner is a strong alkali. Alkali particles do not taste nice at all. That's why toothpaste and indigestion tablets always have a strong flavour added.

Remember

Use the following words to complete the sentences.

litmus   neutral   opposite   alkalis   similar   chemicals   red   indicators

Acids are a family of _____**1**_____ . This means that all acids will do _____**2**_____ chemical changes. Acids turn litmus _____**3**_____ .

_____**4**_____ are the chemical _____**5**_____ of acids. Alkalis turn _____**6**_____ blue.

Chemicals like litmus are _____**7**_____ .

Chemicals can be neither acid or alkaline, these are _____**8**_____ .

Measuring acids

Acid and alkali solutions are not all the same strength. The most dangerous are the concentrated solutions.

The pH scale is used to measure acidity.

Less dangerous acids
citric acid – lemonade malic acid – apples tartaric acid – baking powder ethanoic acid – vinegar
More dangerous laboratory acids
Corrosive
sulphuric acid – car batteries nitric acid – cleaning metals hydrochloric acid – there is a weak harmless solution in the stomach

Table 1

Universal Indicator

You know from Spread 8.1 that litmus goes red with acid and blue with alkali. **Universal Indicator** is a mixture of dyes that goes different colours according to how **concentrated** the acid or alkali in a solution is.

You can buy Universal Indicator solution, or Universal Indicator paper. The paper has been soaked in the solution and dried. The paper is often sold in garden centres.

The pH scale

The **pH scale** is a special scale for measuring acidity. An electronic device can tell you the pH number directly. Or you can get the pH number by using the colour that Universal Indicator turns and matching it to a colour chart.

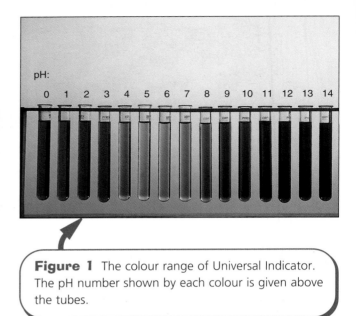

Figure 1 The colour range of Universal Indicator. The pH number shown by each colour is given above the tubes.

Why are acids dangerous?

Acids can be dangerous. When they dissolve in water, the acid compound splits up to make smaller particles. Some of these particles are **hydrogen ions**. They are like fierce animals – they will tear other particles apart. If the substance is acidic, these hydrogen ions are always there. There will be other particles as well – these make up the other half of the acid substance.

The 'hydrogen ion' particles react with metals and rocks to dissolve them. They will also destroy your skin and leave your flesh exposed. This is similar to how a flame burns you. So we talk about 'acid burns' even when acid is cold. Lots of acid particles are a problem but your tough leathery skin can cope with a few acid particles. They will even tickle your taste buds (like in lemonade).

Alkali substances dissolve to produce harmful particles as well – these are called **hydroxide ions**. They are just as fierce as hydrogen ions in acids. They have a harmful effect on organic matter. They will attack grease in your skin, flesh and even wood. They are called **caustic** chemicals.

Questions

Copy and complete this table for Raman. He has done acidity tests on a range of solutions. Some have been tested with Universal Indicator paper and some with a pH meter.

Solution	Reading from pH meter	Colour of Universal Indicator paper
1 black coffee	5	
2 limewater	12	
3 blood	8	
4 sea water		green
5 milk		yellow
6 ammonia solution (surface cleaner)	11	
7 oven cleaner (sodium hydroxide)		purple
8 rust remover (phosphoric acid)		red

9 How strong an acid is phosphoric acid (rust remover)?

10 How strong an alkali is sea water?

11 Name a strong alkali.

12 Name a (very) weak acid.

Questions

13 Copy and complete this table.

Materials harmed by acids	Materials harmed by alkalis

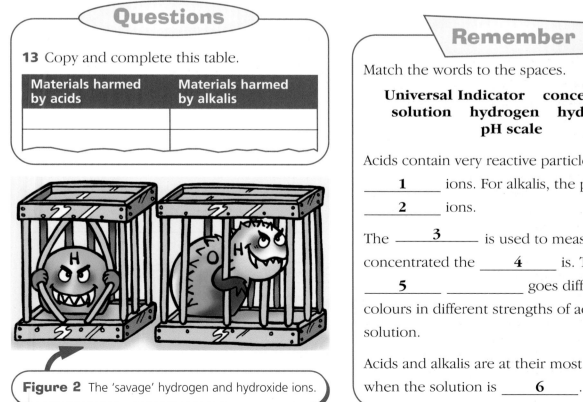

Figure 2 The 'savage' hydrogen and hydroxide ions.

Remember

Match the words to the spaces.

Universal Indicator   concentrated   solution   hydrogen   hydroxide   pH scale

Acids contain very reactive particles called ____1____ ions. For alkalis, the particles are ____2____ ions.

The ____3____ is used to measure how concentrated the ____4____ is. The ____5____ _____ goes different colours in different strengths of acid solution.

Acids and alkalis are at their most dangerous when the solution is ____6____.

Salt and water

Acids react with alkalis. The result is that new water molecules get made. The other particles that are left behind make a new substance called a salt. There are many different sorts of salts.

acid + alkali → salt + water

Acid and alkalis come together to make new substances. The **acidic** hydrogen ions will combine with **alkaline** hydroxide ions. They join together to make **water** particles. So two dangerous particles combine to make a neutral one. This is called **neutralisation**. The other parts of the acid and alkali solution are left behind when this happens. What is left forms a chemical called a **salt**.

Making salts

To show up the change in pH of the solution, you need an indicator or a pH meter. Make the solution exactly neutral, and you will have the salt you want, with no acid or alkali particles.

The coloured indicator can be removed using charcoal. Charcoal is able to absorb coloured materials. Then if you evaporate the water, crystals of salt are left.

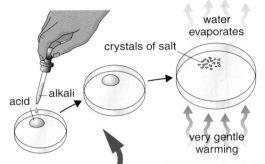

Figure 2 Place two or three drops of acid on a petri dish or glass slide. Add the same amount of alkali. Mix with the end of the dropper and heat very gently. The water evaporates leaving crystals of salt.

The stomach acid problem

Lucy's dad has a problem. His stomach produces too much acid. This rises up and hurts the **oesophagus** that leads from his stomach to his mouth. This is called **heartburn**.

Lucy goes to the pharmacist and gets Milk of Magnesia. Milk of Magnesia has a pH of 9. This reduces the discomfort that Lucy's dad feels. About 5 minutes after swallowing it, he feels better and the pain in his chest has gone.

Questions

1 What are acid particles called?

2 What are alkali particles called?

3 What substance do they join together to make?

4 What happens to the other particles left over?

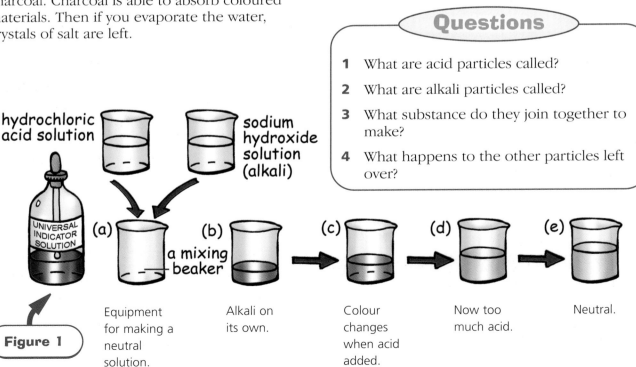

Figure 1

(a) Equipment for making a neutral solution.

(b) Alkali on its own.

(c) Colour changes when acid added.

(d) Now too much acid.

(e) Neutral.

Naming the salt

You can work out the name of the salt from the names of the acid and alkali that made it (see Table 1).

Figure 3

First part of name from alkali		Second part of name from acid
sodium hydroxide makes **'sodium'**	with	hydrochloric acid makes **'chloride'**
potassium hydroxide makes **'potassium'**	with	sulphuric acid makes **'sulphate'**
calcium hydroxide makes **'calcium'**	with	nitric acid makes **'nitrate'**
magnesium hydroxide makes **'magnesium'**	with	ethanoic acid makes **'ethanoate'**

Table 1 Naming salts

Questions

5 Name the salts that are made from:

   a) sulphuric acid and potassium hydroxide

   b) hydrochloric acid and calcium hydroxide

   c) ethanoic acid (vinegar) and magnesium hydroxide.

6 Is Milk of Magnesia an acid or an alkali?

7 Why does it cure heartburn?

8 Stomach acid is hydrochloric acid. What salt is made when the Milk of Magnesia cures heartburn?

9 Why does the pharmacist not use sodium hydroxide (pH of 14) to cure heartburn?

Remember

Use the words below to fill in the spaces.

alkali neutralisation salt particles heartburn name water

Acid ____**1**____ and ____**2**____ particles come together to make ____**3**____. The other bits left behind combine to make a ____**4**____. This process is called ____**5**____. The ____**6**____ of the salt produced depends on which acid and alkali are being used. The salt and water which are made are neutral. That's why weak alkalis help to cure ____**7**____ problems.

Safety with acids

Hazard symbols

Many chemicals are dangerous. They are marked with symbols that tell you how they can harm you. 'Toxic' means it will poison you.

Oxidising
These substances provide oxygen which allows other materials to burn more fiercely.

Highly flammable
These substances easily catch fire.

Toxic
These substances can cause death. They may have their effects when swallowed or breathed in or absorbed through the skin.

Harmful
These substances are similar to toxic substances but less dangerous.

Corrosive
These substances attack and destroy living tissues, including eyes and skin.

Irritant
These substances are not corrosive but can cause reddening or blistering of the skin.

Figure 1 Common hazard symbols

The strongest acid

Aqua regia is the strongest acid known. It is made by mixing one part of concentrated nitric acid with three parts of concentrated hydrochloric acid.

Aqua regia is so strong that it even dissolves gold and platinum. It can't be kept in a metal container because the metal will dissolve. It will even attack glass, so it is kept in a plastic container.

Getting pure gold from jeweller's scrap is the normal use of aqua regia. The scrap is dissolved in the aqua regia. If the acid is treated with other chemicals, the gold is separated out, leaving the more reactive metals, such as silver and brass, in the solution.

The name aqua regia means 'royal water'.

Concentrated acids

These are very dangerous. Especially as both concentrated hydrochloric acid and concentrated nitric acid give off fumes. It is safe to use very small quantities in the laboratory, but usually you would only use concentrated acids inside a fume cupboard.

Hot spot

Concentrated sulphuric acid is a heavy, oily liquid. If you try to dilute it you must be careful. When you mix it with water it transfers energy to its surroundings. The diluted acid solution gets hotter. The acid can even boil.

The rule is to ADD ACID TO WATER. Then only a small amount of energy is released. NEVER add water to the concentrated acid.

Figure 2 This is what concentrated acid does to cloth. Think what it could do to skin!

1 Which do you think is worse: 'toxic' or 'harmful'? Explain why.

2 What is the difference between 'corrosive' and 'irritant'?

3 Why should you not store 'oxidising' and 'highly flammable' chemicals together?

4 Why are the hazard labels bright orange?

5 What is aqua regia used for?

6 Why should you add acid to water when diluting it?

7 'A lab coat is no protection against an acid spill.' Explain why this is true.

8 Draw the hazard labels and test yourself until you know them.

Staying safe

There are three important rules for working with chemicals such as acids and alkalis.

1 **Protect your eyes at all times**
It may not be **your** accident that causes you damage. Your eyes are by far the most easily damaged part of your body.

2 **Never lift chemicals above eye level**
And don't crouch down near benches where there are chemicals.

3 **Treat contact with the skin or eyes with lots of cold water**
Do it immediately, but don't run, as this could cause more accidents. Diluting chemicals helps to make them safe.

Safety equipment

- Safety glasses prevent splashes of acid from getting into the eyes. Goggles are even better because they fit close to the face and no liquid can dribble through.

- Strong rubber gloves and rubber aprons are used by people who work a lot with strong acids. Ordinary clothes will soak up acid and it may come into contact with the skin.

- Ordinary plastic gloves are often used when pouring out acids. The dribbles from the neck can get on to the outside of the bottle.

- Eye-wash bottles of sterile water are kept wherever acids are being used. In larger laboratories there are full immersion showers sticking out of the walls. If anyone suffers a serious acid spill, the nearest people put them under the shower and turn it full on. They may get totally soaked in cold water but the damage from the acid spill is kept to a minimum.

Figure 3 Safety equipment in use in the lab.

9 What is the part of your body that is most easily damaged by chemicals?

10 How can acid dribble down the outside of bottles?

11 Write a set of instructions for using an eye-wash bottle. Check to see if you missed anything out.

Remember

Draw cartoons to illustrate the three safety rules for chemicals to someone who does not understand English very well.

IMPORTANT: Strong alkalis are just as dangerous as acids.

A tale of two acids

Hydrofluoric Acid

Hydrofluoric acid is very dangerous, but the damage it causes does not look serious at first. When hydrofluoric acid touches skin, it passes through into the flesh. The skin is red and not painful at first and it does not look like a typical acid burn. However, over the next few hours the affected area becomes much worse and deep, painful wounds develop. Serious skin damage and tissue loss can occur. The worst cases can lead to death when the fluoride affects the lungs or heart. Hydrofluoric acid is so strong that it can dissolve glass and all metals except for gold.

Citric acid

Do you like sherbet lemons? Their nice sour taste is from citric acid and the fizz is the acid reacting with bicarb.

A property of any acid is a sour taste. Citric acid is the taste in lemonade and other fizzy drinks. We can drink this acid because it is WEAK. If it was a strong acid it would probably take out a couple teeth as we gulped it down!

Citric acid is used to prevent bad smells in foodstuffs as they go off. Citric acid is used as an antioxidant in food such as butter. A tiny amount of citric acid is added to oils to stop them from smelling. Citric acid is also used in many medicines, including some which cure worms, stop blood clotting and make you go to the toilet regularly.

Glass bowl etched by hydrofluoric acid.

Sherbet lemons.

Activity

Hydrofluoric acid and citric acid seem to be very different but they belong to the same family of chemicals.

Draw two cartoon posters to show:

- the dangers of hydrofluoric acid
- the uses of citric acid.

Use a search engine on the web to learn more.

Use one of these phrases for an internet search, then write 50 words that sum up what you found out.

- Acids and tooth decay
- Acid spillage and safety
- Dangerous alkalis – oven cleaner

Electric circuits

Opener Activity
Circuit control

A **battery** can supply **energy** to a **circuit**. There must be a loop of wire and circuit components like lamps. The loop should go from the battery and all the way back to the battery again. This makes a complete circuit.

Most circuits have **switches** to control them. We can use special symbols for batteries, switches and other components, so we don't have to be brilliant artists to draw diagrams of circuits.

Not bad, if I say so myself!

Activity

Circuit symbols

We use symbols a lot. Here are some examples:

1 How many of the symbols can you recognise straight away?

2 Copy the electrical symbols and write a label for each one to say what it is meant to show.

3 You could design a set of symbols for:
- food and drink you might choose for breakfast
- ways you could travel to school and home again
- different lessons
- what you might have for lunch
- how you feel at different times of day.

Draw some of your symbols in a line to show what a day at school is like.

Energy for life

Lamps and heaters transfer energy into the surroundings when they carry a current.

Figure 1 This baby is in an incubator to stay warm. There is a heater wire in an electric **circuit** in one part of the incubator (not too close to the baby). An electric **current** in the heater wire makes it warm. The wire spreads energy into the surroundings. It keeps the baby warm. For the baby, the wire is a life-saver.

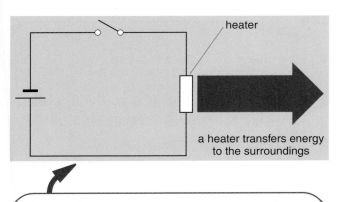

heater

a heater transfers energy to the surroundings

Figure 2 The circuit in the incubator is made up of a battery, a heater wire, a switch and connecting wires. You can make a basic life-saving circuit like this quite easily.

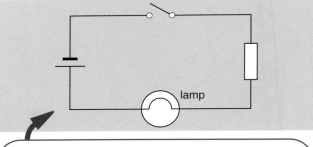

lamp

Figure 3 In a real incubator circuit there might be more **components**. There might be a lamp so that you can see easily when the circuit is on. The lamp and the heater both transfer energy to the surroundings.

It's hard to do a drawing of a circuit exactly as it looks. So we use **symbols** to do simpler drawings.

Part of circuit (component)	Symbol
Battery or cell	
Switch	
Heater or resistor	

Table 1

Setting up circuits

a) To set up a circuit, take a good look at the circuit diagram.

b) Collect the components together and set them out in front of you – in the same order as in the photo.

c) Start at the battery and join the components together with connecting wires.

d) Work your way around the circuit and back to the battery.

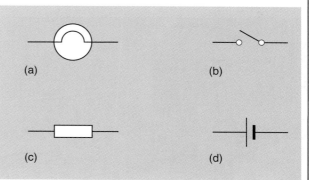

e) It works!

Figure 4

Remember

Match the words to the spaces.

**heater symbols circuits component
lamps out surroundings**

A battery transfers energy into a circuit. A

___**1**___ wire transfers energy ___**2**___

of a circuit and into the ___**3**___.

There are many different kinds of

___**4**___ that you can connect into

electric ___**5**___. ___**6**___ and heater

wires are two kinds of component. When we

draw diagrams we use ___**7**___ for the

different components.

Questions

1 Write down the names of these components.

(a)

(b)

(c)

(d)

2 Draw symbols for:

a) a battery, **b)** a lamp, **c)** a circuit with a battery and a lamp.

3 Where does the energy to warm the baby in the incubator come from?

4 Which of these are designed to transfer energy:

a) a battery, **b)** a heater wire, **c)** a connecting wire?

Current control

You can measure the current in a circuit with an ammeter. The size of the current in a circuit depends on the types of components in the circuit.

Different kinds of circuit

In electricity, the word **current** means the size of the flow around the circuit. Here are some other kinds of flow around circuits.

Figure 1 A flow of people around a circuit.

Figure 2 The boiler, pump, pipes and radiators are components in a central heating circuit. There is a current of hot water all around the circuit. Where the pipes are narrow, there is **resistance** to the current of water.

a)
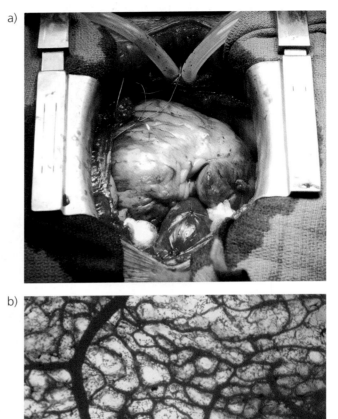

b)

Figure 3 a) This is a human heart during an operation. Inside your body there is a current of blood. Your heart is the pump that keeps the current going in your circuit of blood vessels. In an electric circuit you could think of a battery as a pump. The wire's are a bit like tubes or pipes. b) In some places the blood flows along wide tubes. In other places the tubes are very thin, like in this picture. It's a complicated circuit, with lots of branches.

The incubator circuit on Spread 9.1 is fairly simple. It has quite a few components but it is just a single loop. A single-loop circuit is called a **series circuit**. All the components come one after the other, like a series of TV programmes. It's more like a central heating circuit than a blood circuit.

Measuring the current

You can use an **ammeter** to measure the current in a circuit like the incubator circuit. We measure current in **amps**.

Figure 4 An ammeter connected into a circuit.

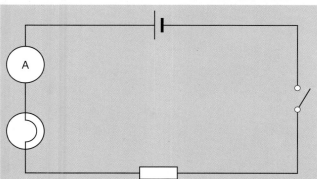

Figure 5 The ammeter goes into the circuit so that the current flows through it. The ammeter becomes part of the loop. It is connected in series with the rest of the circuit. The bigger the current, the further the needle moves along the numbered **scale**.

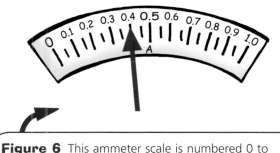

Figure 6 This ammeter scale is numbered 0 to 1.0A. 'A' stands for amps. The **reading** on the ammeter is 0.40A.

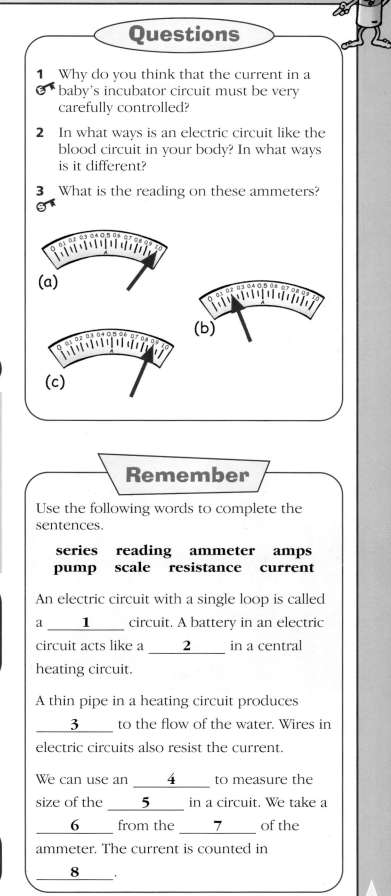

Questions

1 Why do you think that the current in a baby's incubator circuit must be very carefully controlled?

2 In what ways is an electric circuit like the blood circuit in your body? In what ways is it different?

3 What is the reading on these ammeters?

(a)

(b)

(c)

Remember

Use the following words to complete the sentences.

> series   reading   ammeter   amps
> pump   scale   resistance   current

An electric circuit with a single loop is called a ____**1**____ circuit. A battery in an electric circuit acts like a ____**2**____ in a central heating circuit.

A thin pipe in a heating circuit produces ____**3**____ to the flow of the water. Wires in electric circuits also resist the current.

We can use an ____**4**____ to measure the size of the ____**5**____ in a circuit. We take a ____**6**____ from the ____**7**____ of the ammeter. The current is counted in ____**8**____ .

Components and currents

We use ammeters to measure current. The size of a current depends on the components that are in the circuit.

Figure 1 There are many circuits in the instrument panel of an aeroplane.

The circuits in Figure 1 have meters such as ammeters. Ammeters measure electric current. The size of the current depends on what's happening in the circuit. It depends on the components and on how the components are behaving. Components **resist** current. Components have **resistance**. The more resistance they have, the more difficult it is for current to flow. When a component's resistance changes, the current changes.

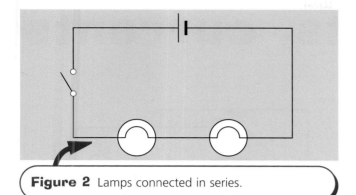

Figure 2 Lamps connected in series.

The lamps in the circuit in Figure 2 are connected one after the other – **in series**. These two lamps resist current *more* strongly than just one lamp. There is *less* current in this circuit than there would be in the circuit with the same battery but only one lamp.

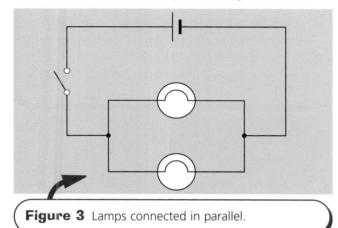

Figure 3 Lamps connected in parallel.

The lamps in Figure 3 are connected side by side – **in parallel**. They both have resistance, but the current has a 'choice' of two routes through the circuit. That means that the two lamps in parallel have *less* resistance than just one lamp. There is *more* current in this circuit than there would be with the same battery and only one lamp.

Questions

1 What happens to the current if the components in a circuit change so that they resist current more?

2 What happens to the current if more lamps are added in series in a circuit?

3 What happens to the current if more lamps are added in parallel with each other?

A water circuit model

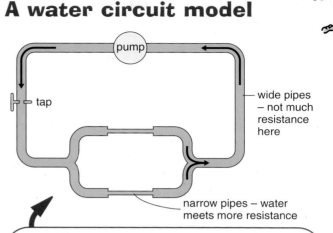

Figure 4 Electric current in a circuit is not exactly like a flow of water along pipes. But in some ways they are similar. A circuit of water pipes needs a pump, and a circuit of wires needs a battery. The water stays in the pipes, but if there are junctions in the circuit then some will go one way and some will go the other. The electric current stays in the wires, and it can also take different routes. The water in the circuit isn't used up, it just goes round and round. Electric current in a circuit isn't used up, it just goes round and round. Narrow pipes can resist a flow of water. Wires can resist electric current.

Remember

Use the following words to complete the sentences.

**components   series   resistance
ammeter   resist   current   circuit
parallel**

Lamps are examples of circuit ____1____.

The number and the type of the components in a ____2____ affect the current. The current can be measured with an ____3____.

Most components ____4____ current. When components are added in ____5____ then the total resistance is bigger. When components are added in ____6____ then the total ____7____ is smaller. The bigger the resistance, the smaller the ____8____ if the battery doesn't change.

Car circuits, currents and fuses

In a single loop (series) circuit, the current is the same everywhere. In a branched (parallel) circuit, the current is split into the different possible routes.

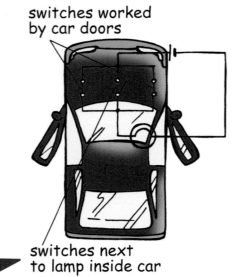

switches worked by car doors

switches next to lamp inside car

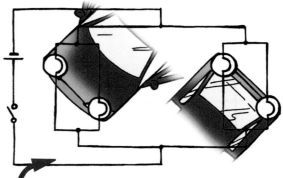

Figure 3 This is a circuit for a car's sidelights. There is only one switch in the circuit, but there are four lamps – two at the front and two at the back. The lamps are connected in parallel. Each one is connected to the battery through the switch. A large current flows through the switch when it is 'on' or 'closed'.

Figure 1 This is a circuit for the light that comes on when you open the front doors of a car. It has three switches – one in each door and one next to the light itself – so that you can also switch it on by hand when the doors are closed. Any one of the switches will switch the light on. The switches are connected **in parallel**.

Strong currents in the thin wires inside light bulbs make the wires white hot. The wires are called **filaments**.

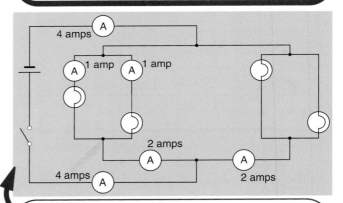

4 amps

A

1 amp 1 amp

A   A

2 amps

4 amps   A   A   2 amps

Figure 4 This circuit has the same arrangements of lamps as Figure 3. The current is split four ways and flows through the lamps. Then the currents from each lamp join back together to return to the battery. The current that goes back to the battery is exactly the same as the current that comes from it.

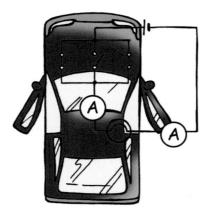

Figure 2 The current that flows into a lamp is the same as the current that flows out. We can show this using ammeters to measure the current.

What if the current is too big?

The filaments inside lamps get so hot that they glow brightly. If the current in the lamps of a car is too big, then the filaments could get hotter still and melt. To prevent this the car's circuit may contain a **fuse**.

A fuse is a small length of thin wire, usually inside a little tube. If the current gets too big the fuse will melt. It's still a nuisance – when the fuse melts the circuit is broken. No more current flows, and the lights go out. But the fuse is cheap and easy to replace. It would cost more to replace the lamps if their filaments melted.

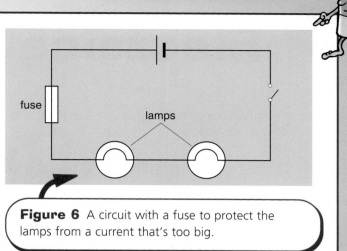

Figure 6 A circuit with a fuse to protect the lamps from a current that's too big.

Questions

1 What is the unit for measuring current?

2 Sketch a circuit diagram for a courtesy light that has switches connected in series. Remember that two switches are operated by the doors. What would you have to do to make the light come on?

3 **a)** In the sidelight circuit (Figure 3), what would happen if one of the lamps stopped working?

   b) Sketch a sidelight circuit with lamps connected in series.

   c) If the lamps were connected in series, what would happen if one of them stopped working?

4 Predict the measurements on the ammeters marked X in each of these circuits.

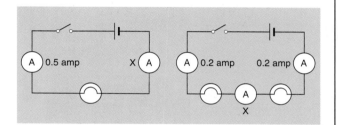

5 What measurement would you expect on the ammeters marked Y in each of these circuits? (The lamps are identical.)

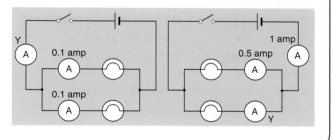

Remember

Solve the anagrams to complete the sentences.

The ampere or 'amp' is the <u>I NUT</u> for measuring current.

The current that flows from a battery is the same as the current that goes <u>K CAB</u> to the battery. When lamps are in <u>SEE SIR</u>, each one has the same current. When lamps are in <u>REAL PALL</u>, the current splits at the junction. The small wires inside the lamps are called <u>FLAT MINES</u>. A small wire that melts when the current gets too big is called a <u>SUE F</u>.

Electrical supplies

The size of a current depends on the number of cells.

Figure 1 Cells and batteries

The objects shown in Figure 1 are **cells**. In everyday language we call them **batteries**. A battery is really a number of cells working together to push current around a circuit. A battery contains cells that are usually connected in series.

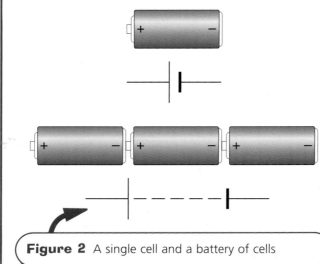

Figure 2 A single cell and a battery of cells

In a circuit, the brightness of the lamp depends on the size of the current. A strong current can make the filament inside a lamp glow white hot. The size of the current depends on two things:

- *What's in the circuit* – for example, how many lamps, what kind of lamp and how they are connected.

- The *number and strength of the cells*.

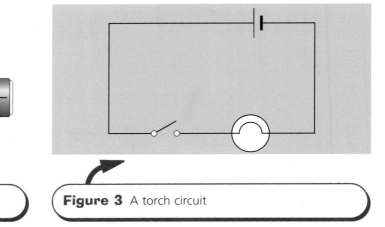

Figure 3 A torch circuit

The torch in Figure 3 has one cell. It pushes a current through the lamp. The current is big enough to make the filament white hot.

Cell measurements

Every cell or battery has a measurement written on it. The unit of the measurement is written as V, which stands for **volts**. A cell for a torch might be a 1.5 volt cell. A car battery has a higher **voltage** – usually 12 volts.

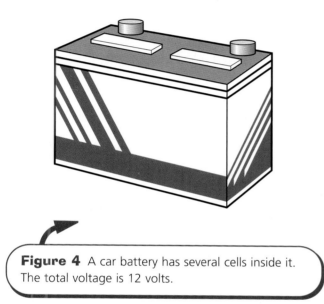

Figure 4 A car battery has several cells inside it. The total voltage is 12 volts.

Electricity at home

The **mains** electricity in your home isn't driven by cells or batteries, but usually by very large generators in power stations. The voltage of the mains supply in your house is 230 volts. That's a big voltage, and it can easily produce big currents. If your body becomes part of a mains circuit then the 230 volts can drive a big current through your body. That could kill you. Mains electricity is dangerous.

When your skin is wet it has less resistance than when it is dry. That means that the mains can make an even bigger current flow across your skin. A big current is more dangerous. That's why you won't find any sockets in your bathroom.

Closer

Your policy on safety

Electricity is dangerous. Electric shocks, or **electrocutions**, kill about 30 people every year in the UK. About another 25 die in fires caused by electrical wiring. There are also thousands of injuries caused by electrical equipment, from computers, to power drills, to washing machines.

So has the time come to ban all electrical equipment? Or should we just carry on using electricity and ignore the deaths?

Another solution would be to use electrical equipment, but to try to reduce the number of accidents. How could we do this?

Activity

1   Obtain more information about electrical hazards and safety. Some good places to start are:

   ● The Health and Safety Executive, HSE, www.hse.gov.uk

   ● The Royal Society for the Prevention of Accidents, ROSPA, www.rospa.com

2   Look at the possible policies for electrical safety, below and decide what you think should happen:

   ● ban electrical equipment

   ● ignore the safety problems

   ● use electrical equipment but reduce accidents as much as possible.

   Which policy would you choose for electrical safety?

3   Produce a four-page leaflet or five-minute PowerPoint presentation to persuade people that your policy is the best one. Your leaflet or presentation should show the advantages of your policy and the disadvantages of the other policies.

4   Make an electricity thinklink map to connect these words together:

   battery   **circuit**   **component**   **current**
                        resistance   **energy**

   Now see where you can fit these words in:

   ammeter   **amp**   **parallel**   **cell**   **energy**
   fuse   **mains**   **series**   **voltage**

CHAPTER 10

Habitats, adaptation and chains

Opener Activity
Habitats, adaptation and chains

Some scientists say that the Earth is warming up, others say that we may have an ice age soon and some scientists claim that increases and decreases in temperature are a natural phenomenon.

Evidence 1

Carbon dioxide CO_2 in the atmosphere is increasing. This might lead to Global warming, the 'greenhouse effect'. CO_2 in the atmosphere prevents heat from escaping like the glass in a greenhouse. The average temperature around the world has been increasing, very slowly over 100s of years.

Evidence 2

CO_2 in the atmosphere has been going up and down for millions of years – at the moment it is going up. Some evidence suggests that levels will keep going up, but it may go down.

Evidence 3

Deforestation (clearing and cutting down trees) is preventing plants from removing excess CO_2 in the atmosphere.

Evidence 4

To produce electricity we often burn coal and oil. This produces CO_2. Many countries have agreed to reduce the amount of CO_2 they produce and have signed an agreement called the Kyoto Treaty. One of the biggest users of energy, the United States of America, refuses to sign.

Evidence 5

Temperatures at the Poles have been going down since the early part of the last century. If global warming was taking place then the temperature at the poles should increase.

Evidence 6

Dr David Bellamy, the botanist, thinks that global warming is a natural thing. The temperature has been going up and down in cycles for millions of years, long before humans and industry existed. He argues that cutting CO_2 emissions will have little or no effect on global warming.

Questions

1 If you had to give an opinion on whether global warming was a 'real' effect or not, how would the evidence above help you?

2 What further information might you need to show that global warming is real?

3 What could we do to help reduce global warming, if it really does exist?

4 In what ways could our 'habitat' change if global warming is actually taking place?

5 How might the types of plants and animals we have in this country change if global warming is real?

6 How might your answer to question 5 be evidence that global warming is real or not?

Is there life on Mars?

Living organisms can adapt successfully to different habitats.

Living organisms are found in many different habitats on Earth, but could life exist on any of the other planets in our solar system? Some scientists believe that life did exist on Mars billions of years ago. They also claim that they have evidence of life on Mars, found as fossil bacteria inside a meteorite believed to have come from Mars.

Percival Lowell (1855–1916), an astronomer, looked at Mars through a telescope and thought that he could see canals on its surface.

Figure 2 Meteorite ALH84001

In 1984, a potato-sized lump of rock was found in the Alice Hills region of Antarctica (Figure 2). It turned out to be a meteorite that had fallen to Earth 13000 years ago. Nobody took much notice of the rock until 1996 when tiny bubbles of trapped gases in the rock were analysed by chemists. They found that the gases were identical to the gases found in the thin atmosphere of Mars. They came to the conclusion that the meteorite was a piece of Mars that had been blasted off the surface. It travelled through space for 16 million years before it landed on Earth.

Figure 1 Mars: the red planet has a dry rocky surface but it also has a white polar cap that is a mixture of ice and dust.

Figure 3 How the meteorite might have landed.

When the scientists looked at the Mars rock they found what looked like tiny fossilised bacteria (Figure 4). These could be the first signs of alien life! Not all scientists agree with this, but the scientists do agree that millions of years ago, Mars had more of an atmosphere than it has today and that water ran over its surface. If you look at the photo of the surface of Mars you can see the channels which water must have run through (Figure 5).

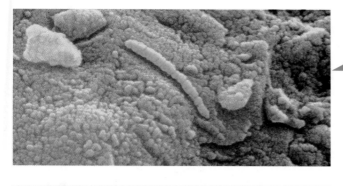

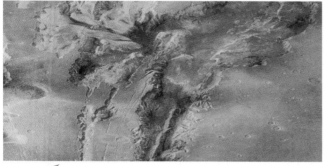

Figure 5 The Valles Marineris on Mars was partly formed by running water.

Lowell's mistake and overactive imagination led him to think that Mars was inhabited by intelligent beings who were capable of planet-wide engineering projects.

	Mars	Earth
diameter	6766 km	12,756 km
length of day	24.62 hours	24 hours
length of year	687 days	365.25 days
strength of gravity	3.7 N/kg	9.81 N/kg
maximum temperature	20°C	50°C
average temperature	−63°C	15°C
minimum temperature	−125°C	−80°C

Atmosphere		
nitrogen	2.7%	78%
oxygen	0.13%	21%
carbon dioxide	95.32%	0.04%
other gases	1.85%	0.96%

Table 1

Figure 4 The first signs of alien life?

Questions

1 Imagine you are a travel writer living on Mars. Write a short piece about life on the planet. Use the information in Table 1 to help you describe how life might be similar or different to living on Earth. Illustrate your article – be creative!

2 Read the following description of a Martian from H.G. Wells' *War of the Worlds*.

'They were huge, round bodies, or rather heads, about four feet in diameter; each body had in front of it a face. This face had no nostrils – indeed the Martians do not seem to have had any sense of smell – but it had a pair of very large, dark coloured eyes, and just beneath this a kind of fleshy beak. In a group around the mouth were 16 slender, almost whiplike tentacles arranged in two bunches of eight each.'

Try to draw a picture of Wells' Martian. Could this Martian really live on Earth?

3 Would a Martian be able to live comfortably on Earth? (*Hint:* think about breathing our atmosphere and what effect the Earth's gravity might have!)

Remember

Use the following words to complete the sentences.

**running water   Solar System   meteorite
little   bacteria   carbon dioxide**

Life may have existed on other planets in the _____**1**_____. Mars has an atmosphere but it contains lots of _____**2**_____ gas, and _____**3**_____ oxygen. Channels made by _____**4**_____ can be seen on Mars. A _____**5**_____ was found which may have had fossilised _____**6**_____ in it.

Jungles, deserts and ice palaces

Living things have been found in all types of places around the world, from deep in the ice at Antarctica to the murky depths of the oceans. Living things adapt to the conditions they find themselves in.

Think about the animals in Figure 1 for a moment. Each of these animals is in the wrong place or **habitat** – the penguin is in the jungle, the scorpion is on the ice of Antarctica, and the gorilla is in the desert.

Questions

1 What problems would each of them have living in these places?

2 How would they have to adapt in order to survive?

Humans adapt to different habitats using technology. We inhabit a large number of places on the Earth, but there are still places where we cannot survive.

3 List some places on Earth where humans cannot survive without special clothes and equipment to help us.

4 Explain how we are able to visit those places; for example, at the top of Mount Everest, climbers need special insulating clothing and extra oxygen to survive.

Moor

Rocky coastline

Woodland

Figure 2 Some different habitats in Britain.

Even in Britain we have different habitats that contain different types of plants and animals which have adapted to where they live. Figure 2 shows some of these habitats.

Scientists called **ecologists** conduct surveys of habitats and list the different types of plants and animals they find there. They also study what happens to habitats when they are damaged by human activity or pollution.

The urban fox

Figure 3 An urban fox raiding a bin for food.

Foxes usually live in the countryside. They eat a wide variety of things including rabbits and other small mammals. Many foxes now live in the cities. They are called urban foxes (Figure 3). Sometimes you can hear them at night – they make a sound like a young baby screaming. This is their mating call. They live off the rubbish that humans put out and on any small mammals they can catch. The urban fox has learned to survive in the cities. People driving home late at night often see urban foxes on the roads.

Look at the two pie charts showing what foxes eat. Think about how the urban foxes have adapted their diet to living in the city.

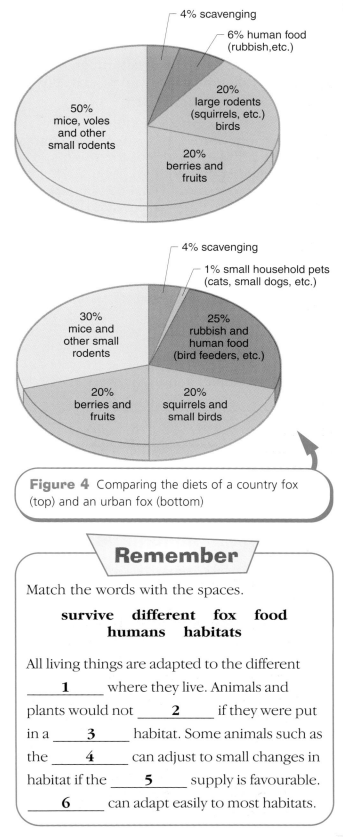

Figure 4 Comparing the diets of a country fox (top) and an urban fox (bottom)

Questions

5   How many different habitats are there in the area where you live and go to school?

6   What sort of animals do you normally see around the school grounds?

7   What sort of animals do you normally see in your garden or near your home?

8   List those features that help the plants and animals live in their habitats. (An example might be that plants living on the ground in woodlands have large green leaves to gather as much light as possible from under the shade of the trees.)

9   Look at Figure 1. Describe which habitat each animal really belongs to and how it is adapted to live there.

Remember

Match the words with the spaces.

**survive   different   fox   food
humans   habitats**

All living things are adapted to the different _____1_____ where they live. Animals and plants would not _____2_____ if they were put in a _____3_____ habitat. Some animals such as the _____4_____ can adjust to small changes in habitat if the _____5_____ supply is favourable. _____6_____ can adapt easily to most habitats.

121

A year in the life of a fox

As a red fox grows up, it goes through a number of different stages as part of its life cycle.

The red fox, *Vulpes vulpes*, is found in many countries, from North and South America to Africa, Asia and all through Europe. It is a common sight in the countryside and is becoming more and more common in our towns and cities.

Foxes have adapted very well to the growth of towns and cities. Not very long ago, the British Isles was mainly farmland with only small towns. At that time, the foxes lived in the open meadowland. As more land has been built on, some foxes have learnt to live among people. They no longer eat meadow creatures, such as rabbits, or steal chickens from farms. Now they get a lot of their food by scavenging in people's dustbins and around houses in towns.

Figure 1 A vixen with her cubs.

How an animal or plant lives, grows, develops and eventually dies can be summed up in what we call a **life cycle**. Read the following account of part of the life cycle of the red fox and answer the questions at the end of page 123.

Figure 2 Worldwide distribution of foxes.

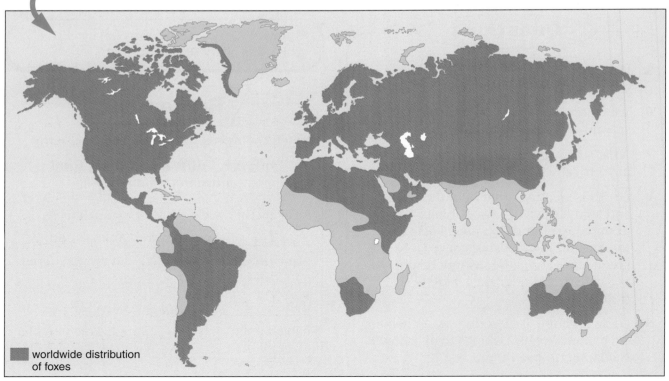

■ worldwide distribution of foxes

During October and November male foxes (dogs) begin to fight among themselves. They mark their territory with scent and by the beginning of the mating season, these marks will have a strong smell. A dog fox and his vixen mate will spend increasingly longer amounts of time with one another to get to know more about each other. Hunting is still a solitary activity, but even then the fox and vixen will call to each other. Red foxes usually only have one mate at a time. They are also well known for staying in the same breeding pairs for several years.

They mate in January or February. Over the following seven or eight weeks the cubs develop in the vixen's womb. Before the cubs are born, the vixen prepares one or more dens in which to give birth. The vixen decides on a den in which to give birth based on factors such as good drainage, access to food and water and how well concealed it is. A few weeks after birth, the cubs may be relocated to other dens several times. As many as 13 cubs may be born, although a typical number is five. The offspring are called cubs, kits, pups or whelps. During the first two weeks, when the mother constantly remains with them to nurse them and keep them warm, she relies on her mate for food for her and the cubs.

The cubs develop quickly. Their bluish-grey eyes are open by their second week and the mother is able to leave them for brief periods of time. By the third week, the cubs can move around and over the next 10 days they begin viciously fighting amongst themselves to establish who is boss! By week four, weaning begins – the cubs start to eat partially-digested food.

The cubs leave the den by their fourth or fifth week. When they first appear, they are a sandy, grey-brown colour. By the second month the cubs are fully weaned, and by the third month they are able to catch small prey such as insects. As summer arrives, the grey coat has been replaced by a reddish one and their blue eyes have turned to a golden colour. At six months, a young red fox is fully grown and has most of the skills it needs to survive.

Questions

1 Draw a time line to show what happens during the life cycle of the red fox. Include as much information as you can about what happens when, from the passage on the left.

2 Where are red foxes found in the world?

3 Why do you think adult male foxes fight during October/November and how do cubs prepare for this as they grow up?

4 What advantage is there in being a solitary hunter?

5 Why might a vixen prepare more than one den in which to give birth?

6 What advantage is there in moving dens after the cubs are born?

7 Why might a young cub's coat colour be different from that of an adult?

8 How have foxes' lives changed since towns spread into the countryside?

9 Where do foxes sometimes look for food for their cubs now?

10 Are foxes a pest or not? Explain your answer.

Remember

Use the following words to complete the sentences.

**survive together environment supply
adapt winter mate food spring**

Animals have to ____1____ to changes in the weather and ____2____. All animals ____3____ and produce young when there is a good ____4____ of food. This is in the ____5____ season. Often they work ____6____ to gather ____7____ and rear their young. The young must be able to ____8____ on their own before ____9____ comes.

Food chains and webs

Food chains and webs show us how energy is transferred from one living organism to another.

Figure 1 A simple food chain

Very few animals eat only one type of food. Most animals, including humans, eat lots of different foods. Many **food chains** can be linked together forming **food webs**.

Stop and think!

The panda only eats bamboo and the koala will only eat eucalyptus leaves.

Why do nearly all other animals eat more than one type of food?

What problems could there be in only eating one food type?

Making food chains and webs is quite a recent idea. In the 1920s Charles Elton, a biologist, was looking at how plants and animals lived and survived in the arctic, at a place called Bear Island. There were few plants and animals for him to study, making it easier for him to see how they lived and fed on each other. He found that the biggest animal, the arctic fox, ate smaller birds, which in turn ate insects that fed off leaves. The plants produced their own food by photosynthesis. He called his description a food chain.

Figure 2 The food chain studied by Elton on Bear Island. Plants → insects → sandpipers → arctic fox

What Charles Elton could see happening at Bear Island also happens in other places, although normally many more plants and animals are involved.

Step number	Name	Plant/animal type
1	**Producer** Something that makes or produces its own food.	green plants
2	**Primary consumer** Primary means first and consumer means to eat, so this level contains animals that eat plants!	insects and herbivores (animals that only eat plants)
3	**Secondary consumer** At this level the animals are usually (but not always!) larger and they will hunt other animals.	usually carnivores (animals that eat other animals) and omnivores (animals that eat both plant and animals)
4	**Decomposer** When plants and animals die, their bodies are broken down and nutrients are put back into the soil. (We don't normally include decomposers in food chains.)	fungi and bacteria

Table 1

Food webs give scientists a better idea of who eats what or whom in real life. Food webs can be very complicated, but like food chains they always start with plants that make their own food.

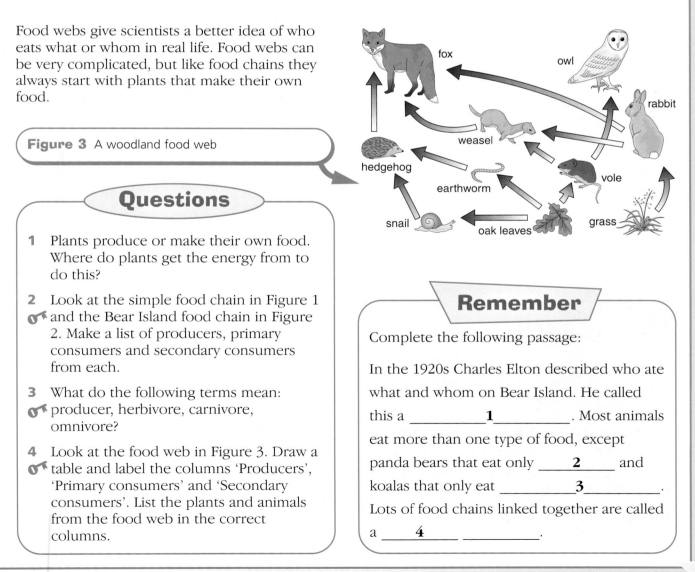

Figure 3 A woodland food web

Questions

1 Plants produce or make their own food. Where do plants get the energy from to do this?

2 Look at the simple food chain in Figure 1 and the Bear Island food chain in Figure 2. Make a list of producers, primary consumers and secondary consumers from each.

3 What do the following terms mean: producer, herbivore, carnivore, omnivore?

4 Look at the food web in Figure 3. Draw a table and label the columns 'Producers', 'Primary consumers' and 'Secondary consumers'. List the plants and animals from the food web in the correct columns.

Remember

Complete the following passage:

In the 1920s Charles Elton described who ate what and whom on Bear Island. He called this a _____1_____. Most animals eat more than one type of food, except panda bears that eat only _____2_____ and koalas that only eat _____3_____. Lots of food chains linked together are called a _____4_____ _____.

Survival!

Some animals and plants have adapted ways of helping them survive predators.

Being part of a food chain or web is dangerous unless you happen to be at the top of the chain. Many plants and animals have had to develop ways of protecting themselves from being eaten by others.

Plants have a number of ways of protecting themselves against being eaten. Some plants are poisonous, others have a bad taste or burn the mouth like chillies and peppers, others have developed to look like poisonous plants although they are not.

Animals have developed many ways of protecting themselves, from armour plating to sharp teeth and claws or camouflage or the ability to outrun other animals.

Questions

Look at the photos of predators and prey on this page. In your exercise book make a list of the animals and plants and say what they have developed either to try and protect them from being eaten or to make them more efficient at catching and eating their prey. Remember it might just be that the way they behave helps them avoid predators!

1 An eagle

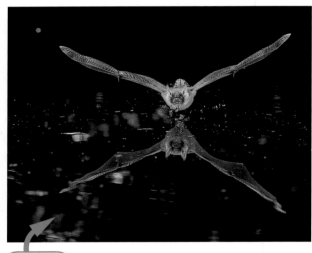

3 A bat

2 Meerkats

4 A spider

5 Chillies

6 A dover sole

8 Cacti

9 A snowshoe hare in summer (left) and winter (right)

7 A stick insect

Remember

Draw pictures of these new animals:

A A mouse that curls into a tight ball covered in sharp spines when it is attacked.

B A rabbit with fur that looks just like long grass, so it can hide when hunted.

C A rodent with an excellent sense of smell but poor eyesight, for hunting at night.

D A bird with a beak and claws for opening very hard nuts.

E A deer with very big ears to hear hunters, and long legs to run fast

Mars may once have had life, but what about now? Could other planets in our solar system have life on them?

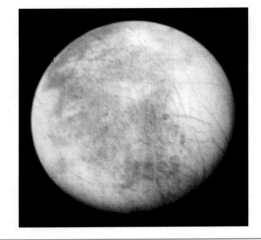

Europa is an icy moon that travels around the planet Jupiter. Beneath a thick icy surface scientists think that there are liquid oceans. Life as we know it needs water and a supply of energy. We get our energy supply from the sun, in the form of heat and light. No light can penetrate the deep oceans of the Earth, so no plants live there. For many years scientists thought that life couldn't exist in such deep waters. Recently we found life near cracks in the ocean crust. Here, life forms get their energy from the superheated water that escapes through the cracks and the bacteria that live in this water. Scientists think that the oceans of Europa could have similar deep sea vents.

Activity

Here are some of the organisms scientists have found near these vents on Earth.

Giant clams that live in this environment measure almost ten inches in length.

1 What do you think life in the oceans of Europa would look like?

2 Draw some pictures of the aliens that live in Europa's oceans. Show how they would

move, catch food and live in an icy ocean that has no light. Keep your pictures. It would be interesting to compare what you have drawn with what we might find one day.

3 Write a short story of your visit to the seas of Europa.

Chemical change

The Fire Service attracts fit young men and women who want to keep the public safe.

Being a firefighter is much more than driving a shiny red fire engine and wearing a smart uniform. To get into the Fire Service you need to be physically fit – and you need to pass exams. A lot of the questions asked are about science, particularly about how substances react and burn!

'There was smoke and roasting hot air all around us. I told Lee I wanted the fire break at least a bulldozer blade wide and be sure to push the uprooted trees away from the cleared area. I told him to be very careful not to push dirt over any burning material. I started off up the ridge, tying plastic ribbon to mark the path of the fire break.'

Here are two questions from a real firefighter exam paper.

A You are in charge of an incident and you decide to use fire-fighting foam. What factors influence the effective use of the foam?

B You are at a road-traffic accident. A road tanker is involved, and it is leaking a liquid that is giving off clouds of vapour. You suspect it is a strong acid. How would you deal with the spill so as not to affect the surrounding area?

Questions

1 Make a short list of some science ideas that a firefighter would use in their job.

2 Why do you think foam is used to fight some sorts of fires?

3 Explain, using a particle model, why the liquid from the tanker is giving off lots of vapour.

4 You decide to soak the acid up with sand mixed with a mild alkali, rather than wash it into the nearby fishing lake. Explain why.

Forest fire

5 What is a fire break?

6 Why do they push the trees away from the fire break?

7 Why are they careful not to cover burning material?

What munches metal?

Most metals react with acids. Hydrogen gas is produced from the acid. The metal gets dissolved and turned into a salt.

Figure 1 Alarm bells, warning sirens – you've seen it on TV. The saliva of the space monster is eating through the deck of the ship and everyone's going to . . .

Is this really true? It's usually something to do with the words **acid** and **metal**. Many metals are attacked by the hydrogen ion particles in acids. The acid dissolves the metal and **hydrogen** gas is produced from the acid. The laboratory apparatus is made of glass because acids would attack metal equipment.

But the science fiction story is not totally true. Most metals react slowly with acids and as the acid dissolves the metal, the acid gets **neutralised** itself.

Camel urine is a liquid that is very corrosive to aeroplanes. If aeroplanes are carrying camels, their urine will eat through the metal floor!

Questions

1 What happens when the magnesium is first put in the acid?

2 What happens to the solid magnesium metal in the end?

Testing a gas to see if it is hydrogen

You have to take great care. Only try this with a test tube full of the gas.

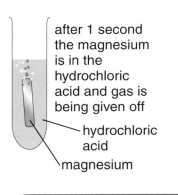

after 1 second the magnesium is in the hydrochloric acid and gas is being given off
— hydrochloric acid
— magnesium

after 10 seconds the magnesium is considerably eaten away but is still fizzing

after 20 seconds the magnesium has gone

Figure 2 The reaction between magnesium and hydrochloric acid.

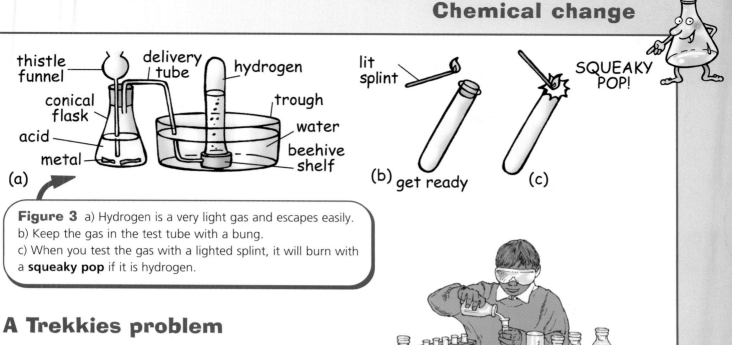

Figure 3 a) Hydrogen is a very light gas and escapes easily.
b) Keep the gas in the test tube with a bung.
c) When you test the gas with a lighted splint, it will burn with a **squeaky pop** if it is hydrogen.

A Trekkies problem

Baghi was sure that Star Trek was true and all metals would dissolve in acid. He tried four metals and two acids. He chose hydrochloric acid and sulphuric acid. He knew these were strong acids. His results are shown in Table 1.

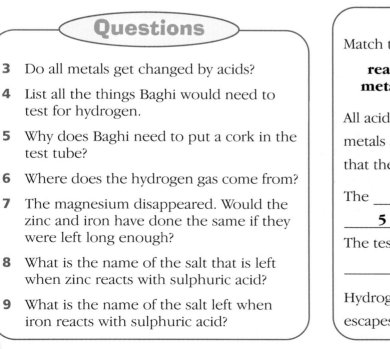

Figure 4 Baghi testing acids in the lab.

Metal	Hydrochloric acid	Sulphuric acid
zinc	fizzed steadily	fizzed steadily
copper	nothing happened	nothing happened
magnesium	fizzed very quickly and dissolved	fizzed very quickly and dissolved
iron	fizzed slowly	fizzed slowly

Table 1 Baghi's results

Questions

3 Do all metals get changed by acids?

4 List all the things Baghi would need to test for hydrogen.

5 Why does Baghi need to put a cork in the test tube?

6 Where does the hydrogen gas come from?

7 The magnesium disappeared. Would the zinc and iron have done the same if they were left long enough?

8 What is the name of the salt that is left when zinc reacts with sulphuric acid?

9 What is the name of the salt left when iron reacts with sulphuric acid?

Remember

Match the words to the spaces.

**react   acids   copper   hydrogen
metals   tube   squeaky pop   light**

All acids ____1____ with most metals. Some metals such as ____2____ are so unreactive that they do not react with ____3____.

The ____4____ get dissolved and ____5____ gas is produced from the acid. The test for hydrogen is it burns with a ____6____.

Hydrogen is a very ____7____ gas. It escapes from a test ____8____ very easily.

131

Making a fizz

Acid plus a carbonate makes a salt plus water, plus a fizz of carbon dioxide gas.

calcium carbonate	+	hydrochloric acid	→	calcium chloride (SALT)	+	water	+	carbon dioxide (GAS)

Marble is a beautiful stone, it is used to make statues and grand buildings. Marble is made from a chemical called **calcium carbonate**. It gets attacked by acids. Acidic particles are savage. They rip the calcium carbonate particles in the rock apart to make new substances. One of the new substances has particles that move so rapidly that it is a gas. The gas is **carbon dioxide**.

All carbonates will neutralise acids. The acidic particles rip the carbonates up, but are chemically changed when they do it. The bits left over make a **salt**. The type of salt depends on which carbonate and which acid were used.

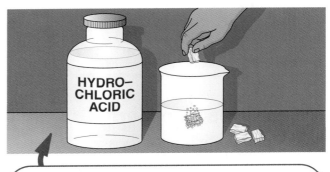

Figure 1 When the piece of marble is added to the hydrochloric acid it fizzes as carbon dioxide is released.

Testing for carbon dioxide

Carbon dioxide is the fizz gas that you see when marble is added to any acid. It is colourless and it does not smell – so how can you tell it is carbon dioxide?

Put about 5 cm^3 of **limewater** (calcium hydroxide solution) into a test tube. Carbon dioxide is a heavy gas so it can be poured into the test tube like in Figure 2. Put your thumb over the test tube and shake it. Carbon dioxide gas will make the limewater go white and milky.

Questions

1 What do you see when an acid reacts with marble?
2 What is the name of the gas given off?
3 What happens to the acid particles?
4 Many marble statues have been damaged by acid pollution. Explain why.

Figure 2 Using limewater to test for carbon dioxide.

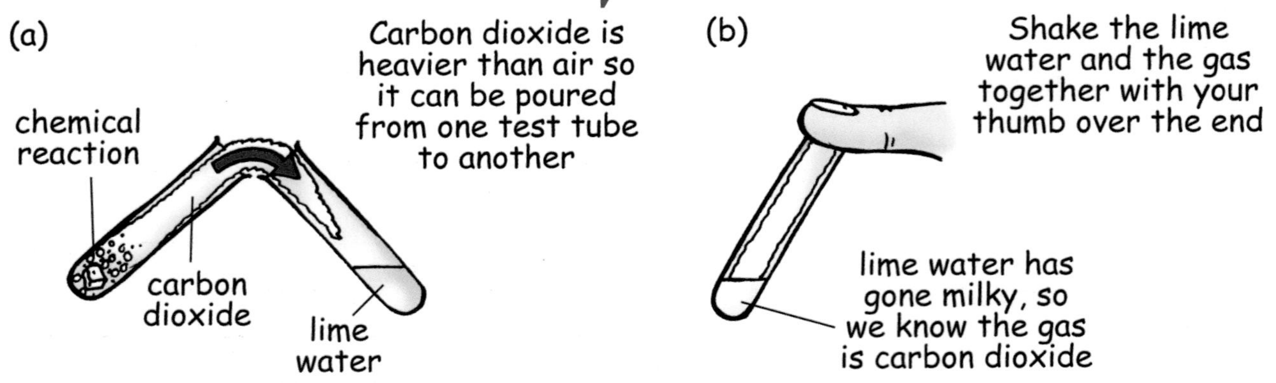

(a) chemical reaction — carbon dioxide — lime water

Carbon dioxide is heavier than air so it can be poured from one test tube to another

(b) Shake the lime water and the gas together with your thumb over the end

lime water has gone milky, so we know the gas is carbon dioxide

Is there a pattern?

Luis knew there was a whole range of chemical substances, all of which had names ending in '-ate' – there were carbonates, sulphates, nitrates. He tested some of them with acid. He asked his teacher first, who told him it was safe so long as he wore goggles on his eyes. His results are shown in Table 1.

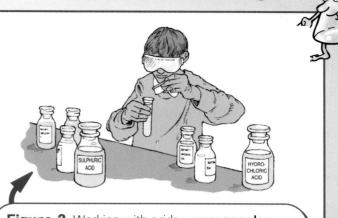

Figure 3 Working with acids – wear **goggles** and **be careful**!

Substance	What he saw when he added acid	Result of test with limewater
magnesium carbonate	fizz of gas and substance dissolved	limewater turned milky
magnesium sulphate	substance dissolved	no effect
iron carbonate (brown)	fizz of gas and substance dissolved	limewater turned milky
iron nitrate	substance dissolved	no effect
copper carbonate	fizz of gas and substance dissolved	limewater turned milky
copper nitrate	substance dissolved	no effect
sodium carbonate	fizz of gas and substance dissolved	limewater turned milky
sodium sulfate	substance dissolved	no effect

Table 1 Luis' results

Questions

5 Make a list of what you need to do these tests.

6 Write a step-by-step method for doing the tests.

7 How do you test a gas to see if it is carbon dioxide?

8 How many of the substances were carbonates?

9 How many of the substances gave off carbon dioxide?

10 Were they the same ones?

11 Luis used sulpuric acid. Write word equations for the reaction with magnesuim carbonate and copper carbonate.

Remember

Fill the missing answers into the word grid and find the hidden word.

Limewater goes _____

Carbonates react with _____

Using acid, you must be _____

The fizz substances are _____

Use _____ water in the test

Put the limewater in a _____ tube

Word grid

A nice change

Some materials just melt or boil when heated. Others change permanently – these are chemical changes.

Pancakes

Figure 1 In the café Mandy is making pancakes.

1 Mandy mixes the egg, flour and milk until creamy smooth. She then adds salt to taste.

2 She melts a little fat into a hot pan.

3 She pours in about 40 cm³ of the mixture and cooks it for about 30 seconds on each side.

Mandy can see different changes take place as she makes the pancakes.

- When she heats the fat it loses its shape and turns into a liquid.

- When she cooks the pancake mix, it turns from a liquid to a solid and keeps its shape.

These are two different types of **change**.

When fat is heated it **melts**. When it cools again it **solidifies**. This can happen over and over again. The solid fat is able to change into a liquid when it is hot and change back again when it cools. This is called a **physical change**.

But when pancake mix is heated, the liquid turns into a solid shape. When it cools, it stays permanently in this shape. This is an example of a **chemical change**.

The pancake mixture has been heated to change it into something nicer to eat.

Cooking changes

Lots of chemical changes happen in cooking.

Figure 2 Sugar is heated to make caramel toffee.

Figure 3 Bread is grilled to make toast.

Figure 4 Egg is cooked and goes solid.

In your answers try to use scientific words like solid or liquid, cloudy or clear.

1 a) Describe what you see when cooking fat is solid.

b) What does it look like when it is liquid?

2 a) Describe what pancake mix looks like before it is cooked.

b) What does it look like after it is cooked?

3 a) Think of three other cooking changes. Describe what the food looks like before and after cooking.

b) Has the food changed permanently?

4 Copy the diagram of the water cycle. Label it and colour it in.

5 What makes the water evaporate from the sea?

6 Why does the water vapour become snow?

7 Does the rain contain salt? Explain your answer.

8 Why does 'global warming' make the weather wetter?

The water cycle

The **water cycle** is about how the water in our environment makes rain, lakes and seas. There are lots of 'physical changes' involved in this cycle.

The water becomes solid (ice), liquid (water) and gas (water vapour) but it never stops being the same substance.

Remember

Match the words to the spaces.

melt   substance   cooking   chemical   change   physical

When we heat substances they can ___1___. If they just ___2___ or evaporate, this is a ___3___ change.

But sometimes the substance changes into a different ___4___. This is a ___5___ change. ___6___ causes chemical changes.

Figure 5 The water cycle

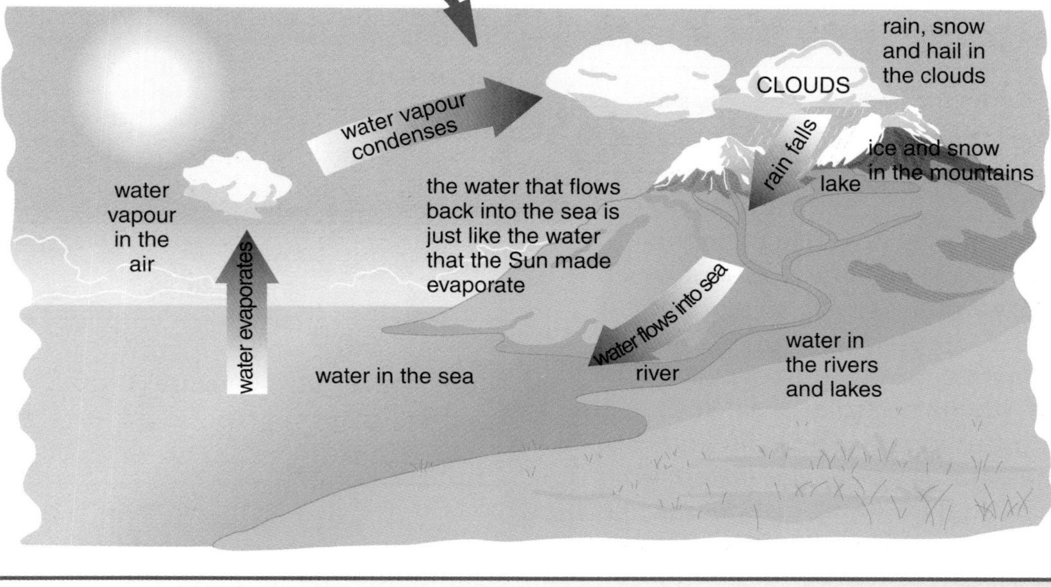

135

Fire

When many substances react with oxygen in the air, they transfer energy as heating and light. This is called burning.

Fire has been our friend for over 400 000 years. Fire kept us warm. It frightened away wild animals.

Fire is a fuel reacting with oxygen in the air. The flames you can see are gases from the fuel mixing and reacting with the air. When they do this you get lots of heat. This is called an **oxidation reaction**. Oxygen combines with the fuel to make new substances. These are called **oxides**. Some particles glow in the flames, giving the flames their yellow colour. A yellow Bunsen flame has soot in it. The soot glows as it burns.

Figure 1 Fumes are produced when you strike a match.

We start fires with matches. Matches contain phosphorus. Phosphorus is an element which is 'greedy' for oxygen. A German soldier named Hening Brand discovered phosphorus in 1669. He was evaporating urine to discover a way of making gold! When you strike a match the phosphorus burns rapidly. The white fumes and smell are phosphorus oxide. The phosphorus has been oxidised. Phosphorus oxide is acidic. It makes you cough if you breathe it in.

Questions

1 What other substance is needed for a fuel to burn?

2 What is happening when you see flames?

3 What makes a Bunsen flame yellow sometimes?

4 What burns when matches are struck?

5 What substance is the smell of matches?

6 Write a word equation for burning matches.

7 Matches don't burn unless they get a bit of energy to start the reaction. Explain how this happens.

Where does the energy come from?

Fuels are made of molecules. The atoms that make up these molecules react with oxygen. The new molecules made in the chemical change contain less stored energy than the fuel molecules. This is because some energy is released. Normally it is released by heating but it could also be released as electricity or light.

Equations

This is a word equation for the reaction at a Bunsen flame.

Methane + oxygen →
      carbon dioxide + water vapour

This is the formula equation for the same reaction.

$$CH_4 + 2O_2 \rightarrow CO_2 + 2H_2O$$

The fuel we use as bottled gas is called **propane**. It is made of simple molecules containing three carbon atoms and eight hydrogen atoms. It needs five molecules of oxygen to 'burn' one molecule of methane.

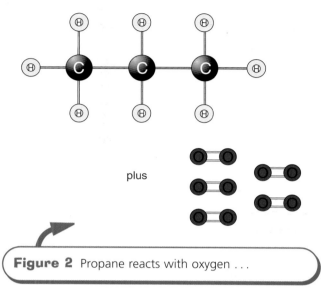

plus

Figure 2 Propane reacts with oxygen . . .

When the propane and oxygen have reacted (burnt) the atoms change partners and make new molecules. They make carbon dioxide and water molecules.

plus

Figure 3 . . . to produce carbon dioxide and water

Exactly the same atoms are there. They have just swapped round to make **bonds** with new partners. Each of these bonds has an 'energy' value. The energy value of the bonds in carbon dioxide and water molecules adds up to less than the value of the bonds in propane and oxygen.

Figure 4 A propane gas burner

Questions

8 Copy and fill in this table using information from Figures 4 and 5.

Type of atom	Number of atoms before reaction (Figure 2)	Number of atoms after reaction (Figure 3)
carbon		
hydrogen		
oxygen		

9 What is the formula for propane?

10 What is the formula of an oxygen molecule?

11 Write a word equation for the propane/oxygen reaction and underneath write a formula equation for the reaction.

Remember

Read, copy and learn the following:

Chemical changes usually result in the transfer of energy.
Taking molecules apart takes in energy.
Putting molecules together gives out energy.
Fuels transfer energy as heat and light when they burn.

Burning hot

Burning fuels transfer energy by heating and lighting the surroundings.

Figure 1 Burning fuels to release energy.

Fuels

Fuels like coal, oil and gas are substances that release energy when we burn them. We must make sure we do this in a controlled, safe way. Different fuels are often burned in different ways. For example wood can be burned on an open fire, but petrol is usually burned inside a car engine.

When fuels burn they use up oxygen and form new substances. The substances produced depend on the elements in the fuel. At the same time energy is released into the surroundings. For example when natural gas is burned in air on a gas hob, the energy released is used to cook our food.

Fuels like coal, gas and oil are **fossil fuels**. They are found in rocks underground. They were made over millions of years from the remains of dead animals and plants. Because new substances are made, this is a **chemical change**.

Reactions like this, where energy is released from fuels, are called **combustion** reactions.

Questions

1 Make a list of three fuels that are used

   a) at home

   b) in cars

   c) in industry.

2 What gas from the air is used in burning fuels?

3 What is made of the energy released

   a) when petrol is burned in car engines?

   b) when fuel is burned in a space rocket?

4 Where did fossil fuels come from?

5 What new substances are made when a fossil fuel burns?

6 Which fossil fuel does a Bunsen burner burn?

Fighting fire

Home fires kill about 500 people a year in Britain. Most of these fires begin accidentally, but how does it happen? You can get barbecue charcoal that is easy to light in supermarkets. But it doesn't go up in flames in the store. Forests take many years to grow and yet every so often you read about forest fires.

A fire needs three things to get it going:

- fuel
- oxygen
- a high temperature

These are often shown as the fire triangle.

fossil fuel + oxygen → carbon dioxide + water + energy transfer

Chemical change

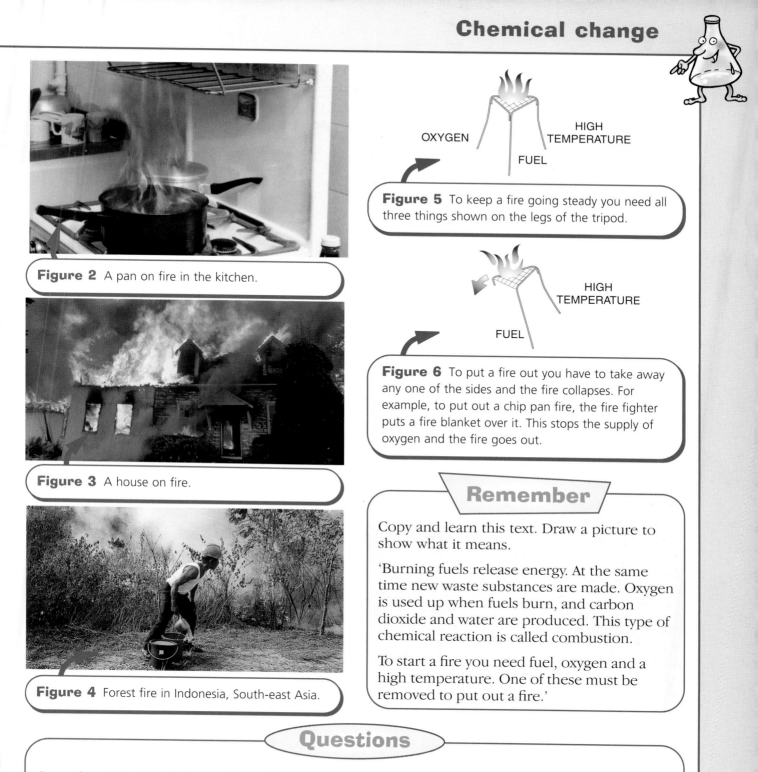

Figure 2 A pan on fire in the kitchen.

Figure 3 A house on fire.

Figure 4 Forest fire in Indonesia, South-east Asia.

OXYGEN

HIGH TEMPERATURE

FUEL

Figure 5 To keep a fire going steady you need all three things shown on the legs of the tripod.

HIGH TEMPERATURE

FUEL

Figure 6 To put a fire out you have to take away any one of the sides and the fire collapses. For example, to put out a chip pan fire, the fire fighter puts a fire blanket over it. This stops the supply of oxygen and the fire goes out.

Remember

Copy and learn this text. Draw a picture to show what it means.

'Burning fuels release energy. At the same time new waste substances are made. Oxygen is used up when fuels burn, and carbon dioxide and water are produced. This type of chemical reaction is called combustion.

To start a fire you need fuel, oxygen and a high temperature. One of these must be removed to put out a fire.'

Questions

Copy the table. Match the collapsed fire triangles to these ideas for fire fighting.

Method to stop fire	How does the fire triangle collapse?
7 Pour water on a charcoal barbecue	
8 Cut down the trees in the path of a forest fire	The fire stops because it runs out of fuel
9 Turn off the gas if there is an accident in the laboratory	
10 For a person whose clothes are on fire, wrap them in a blanket or large coat	

Closer

Activity

Fizz

Carbon dioxide is the fizz in bottled water. Three friends took a bottle of fizzy water out of the fridge. They left the top off and tested the water with a pH meter every ten minutes. They also recorded the mass and temperature.

Here are their results.

Table 1

Time/Minutes	Temp (°C)	Ph
0	0	3.0
10	7	4.2
20	14	5.4
30	18	6.1
40	20	6.5
50	20	6.5

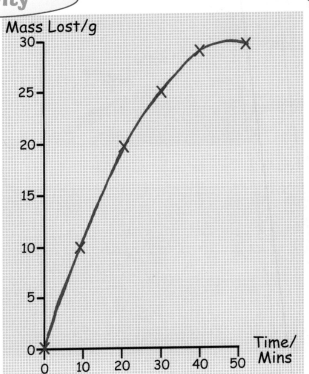

Jack: The gas has escaped so the liquid got lighter.

Venus: The carbon dioxide gas makes the fizzy water acidic.

Thierry: Gas doesn't stay dissolved so much when water gets hotter.

1 How could you test the gas to prove it was carbon dioxide and not hydrogen?

2 Plot a graph or bar chart of the data in the two tables. Write a sentence to explain the link between the two sets of data.

3 Explain, in your own words, what the graph of temperature and mass of the water bottle shows you.

4 What evidence is there to support Jack's conclusion? Explain why you agree with him.

5 What evidence is there to support Venus's conclusion? Explain why you agree with her.

6 What evidence is there to support Thierry's conclusion? Explain why you agree with him.

The Solar System

Opener Activity
So what's your idea?

Activity

Sometimes we are in daylight and sometimes we are in darkness. That's obvious. But how does it happen?

1 Look at the list below and try to decide how each event happens. Make a list or a table and write down what you think. It might also help to discuss your ideas. Don't worry if you are not very sure about your ideas. Even if you make a guess it gives you something to think about. You could mark your ideas as 'confident' or 'not confident'.

- We have day and night (daylight and darkness). How does that happen?
- The Moon sometimes looks round, sometimes it looks like a thin crescent, and sometimes in between. How does that happen?
- The Sun always looks round and bright except during a solar eclipse. Why doesn't it change like the Moon does?

- Why does a solar eclipse make the Sun's shape change?
- We have summer and winter. How does that happen?
- The stars stay in the same patterns all of the time. Why?
- Planets do not stay in fixed patterns. They move across the patterns of the stars. Why are the planets different?
- Nobody has ever been to another planet. Why not?
- It's very, very unlikely that anybody will ever travel close to a star outside the Solar System. Why not?

2 Check your ideas after you've studied the Solar System. See how many of your ideas have changed.

3 Should you have fixed ideas or is it better to change your ideas when you learn more?

Sunshine and shadows

The Sun is the source of light that gives us daylight. Light travels out in all directions in straight lines from the Sun, and some of it reaches the Earth.

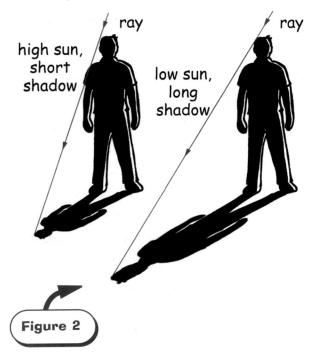

Figure 1 People make shadows

Light can't travel through people. It can't travel around them, either. People, dogs and other objects block the sunlight and make shadows on the ground. We can make diagrams to show the straight pathways of light. The pathways are called **rays**.

ray   ray

high sun, short shadow   low sun, long shadow

Figure 2

Moonshadows

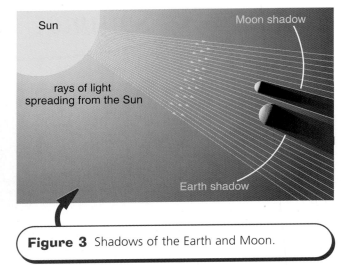

Sun

rays of light spreading from the Sun

Moon shadow

Earth shadow

Figure 3 Shadows of the Earth and Moon.

The Sun shines its brilliant light on the Earth and the Moon. The Earth and the Moon make huge shadows. An astronaut going around the Earth goes in and out of its shadow.

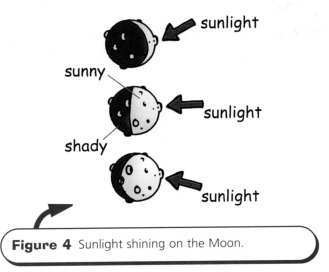

sunlight

sunny

sunlight

shady

sunlight

Figure 4 Sunlight shining on the Moon.

Sunlight can only shine on half of the Moon at a time. So half of the Moon is in its own shadow. From Earth we see the sunny part. Sometimes we see all of the sunny side of the Moon and then we call it a **Full Moon**. Sometimes we see the shady side of the Moon, and perhaps just a thin slice of the sunny side. Then we call it a **New Moon**. The time from one New Moon to the next one is always just less than a month.

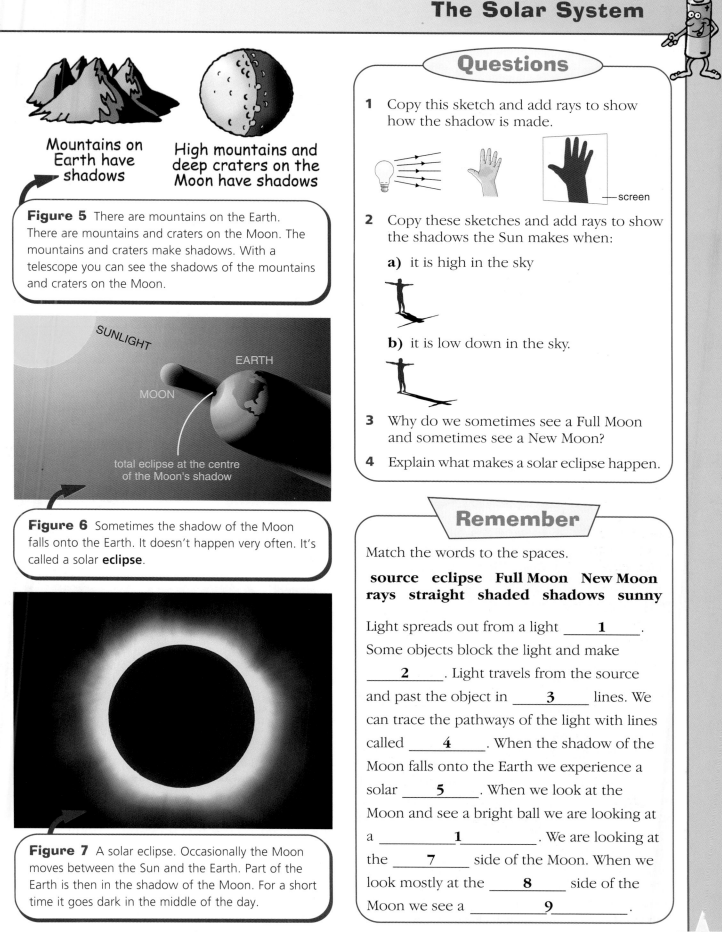

Mountains on Earth have shadows

High mountains and deep craters on the Moon have shadows

Figure 5 There are mountains on the Earth. There are mountains and craters on the Moon. The mountains and craters make shadows. With a telescope you can see the shadows of the mountains and craters on the Moon.

SUNLIGHT

EARTH

MOON

total eclipse at the centre of the Moon's shadow

Figure 6 Sometimes the shadow of the Moon falls onto the Earth. It doesn't happen very often. It's called a solar **eclipse**.

Figure 7 A solar eclipse. Occasionally the Moon moves between the Sun and the Earth. Part of the Earth is then in the shadow of the Moon. For a short time it goes dark in the middle of the day.

Questions

1 Copy this sketch and add rays to show how the shadow is made.

—screen

2 Copy these sketches and add rays to show the shadows the Sun makes when:

a) it is high in the sky

b) it is low down in the sky.

3 Why do we sometimes see a Full Moon and sometimes see a New Moon?

4 Explain what makes a solar eclipse happen.

Remember

Match the words to the spaces.

source   eclipse   Full Moon   New Moon rays   straight   shaded   shadows   sunny

Light spreads out from a light _____**1**_____. Some objects block the light and make _____**2**_____. Light travels from the source and past the object in _____**3**_____ lines. We can trace the pathways of the light with lines called _____**4**_____. When the shadow of the Moon falls onto the Earth we experience a solar _____**5**_____. When we look at the Moon and see a bright ball we are looking at a _____**1**_____. We are looking at the _____**7**_____ side of the Moon. When we look mostly at the _____**8**_____ side of the Moon we see a _____**9**_____.

Escape from the Earth

The force of gravity is a force that can act at a distance. Large objects like the Earth and the Sun exert large forces of gravity.

Stars and planets pull strongly on all other objects that are near to them. The force acts on objects that are not touching. We call it the force of **gravity**.

Gravity is a strong part of our everyday lives. It's strange to think that our lives would be very different if the force of gravity were like electric and magnetic forces. Those forces can attract or repel. Gravity only attracts. Try to imagine what life would be like if the Earth attracted some objects and repelled other objects.

Figure 2 Laika, the first dog in space.

Astronauts escape from the Earth's atmosphere into space. But they *don't* escape from the Earth's gravity. Gravity holds them in **orbit** around the Earth.

Figure 1 Life would be different if gravity could repel.

Figure 3 Above the atmosphere, in empty space. But gravity still pulls on this astronaut. The astronaut keeps going round and round the Earth.

The Earth is a huge ball with a surface that's covered in rock and water. We spend all of our lives on it. Only a few animals and a few people have been outside the Earth's **atmosphere** and into space. The atmosphere is a layer of air all around the Earth. The first animal to do this was Laika, a Russian dog. In 1957, she was launched up through the Earth's atmosphere into the empty space above. The Russians wanted to see if an animal could survive the journey. There was no air to breathe outside her spacecraft, so the spacecraft had to carry air to keep her alive.

Only a very few people have ever set foot anywhere except on Earth. Neil Armstrong was the first, in 1969, when he stepped on to the Moon. The Moon has its own gravity. But since the Moon is smaller than the Earth, its gravity is weaker. The Earth and the Moon pull on each other, so that they orbit around each other and travel together through space.

Figure 4 The astronaut Buzz Aldrin walking on the Moon. The Moon's own gravity holds him to the surface.

Figure 5 As the Moon is smaller than the Earth, its gravity is not as strong.

Only in stories have people travelled so far that they escaped from the pull of the gravity of the Earth and the Moon.

Figure 6 Adventure in space – away from the force of gravity of any star or planet.

Questions

1 a) What is the Earth's atmosphere?

   b) Why did Laika's space capsule need to carry an air supply?

2 a) Have you ever escaped from the surface of the Earth?

   b) Do you think that you will ever escape from the Earth's atmosphere?

3 a) Why is the gravity of the Moon weaker than the gravity of the Earth?

   b) Describe what you think it would feel like to walk on the Moon, like Neil Armstrong did.

4 Draw a picture of the launch of a space mission or a satellite. Show the rocket motors working.

5 Write about what it would be like to be an astronaut being launched.

Remember

Unscramble the anagram words to complete the spaces in the passage.

All large objects like stars and planets exert a force of <u>GRAVY IT</u>. The force is always <u>TIE RAT V CAT</u>. The bigger the object, the <u>BRIG EG</u> the force.

We are held on the <u>HES ART</u> surface by its strong force of gravity. Nobody has ever escaped completely from the influence of the Earth's gravity. Some people have been above the <u>AT HER POEMS</u> of the Earth, where there is no air.

Planet hopping

The Sun is a huge star at the centre of a system of planets called the Solar System. The Earth is one of these planets. The Sun's strong force of gravity keeps the planets in orbit around the Sun.

A long time ago, in 1977, two new spacecraft were launched into space. They were called Voyager 1 and Voyager 2. They are still travelling today. On their journeys they have been past many planets and their moons. Now they are so far away from the Earth and the Sun that there are no more planets for them to visit. They have become the first human-made objects to escape from the **Solar System**.

The Sun is by far the largest object in the Solar System. The Sun is at the centre – it is the gravity of the Sun that holds the planets in their orbits. Without this force of gravity, the Earth and the other planets would escape from the Sun. If the Earth escaped then we would lose the warmth of the Sun. We would not receive the energy that plants need to grow, and we would starve and freeze in darkness.

Figure 1 The picture shows how the sizes of the planets compare. In reality, they don't lie in such a straight line and the distances between them are HUGE. The planets' moons are not shown. A small planet called Sedna exists beyond the orbit of Pluto.

Martian sunset – Mars is further from the Sun than the Earth is so the Sun looks smaller from Mars. The picture was taken by the Viking space mission.

The Sun's force of gravity on an object gets weaker as it gets further from the Sun. Voyager 1 and 2 have now gone so far away that the Sun exerts hardly any pull at all. There are no stars other than the Sun anywhere near the Solar System. Some distant stars also have their own system of planets in orbit around them.

moons of Jupiter

Jupiter is the biggest planet. It is a very different world from our own planet Earth. It is a ball of gas, and because it 's so big, its gravity is very strong.

Io is a rocky moon in orbit around Jupiter. It has active volcanoes, just like the Earth.

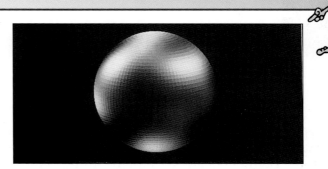

Pluto is a small planet a long way from the Sun. The Sun's light is weak on Pluto, so it is a very cold planet. This picture was taken by the Hubble Space Telescope.

Questions

1   If the Sun is just a star, why does it look much bigger than other stars?

2   During their long journeys, what has happened to the strength of the Sun's gravity pulling on Voyager 1 and 2?

3   a) Why are there no people travelling on board Voyager 1 or 2?

   b) Do you think that people will go that far one day?

Remember

Complete the sentences below using the following words.

Sun   orbit   stars   distances   planet   gravity

The force of gravity acts over very large

_____1_____ . It is strongest close to a star or

_____2_____ , and gets gradually weaker as

you move away.

The _____3_____ is a star. The Earth and the

other planets are in _____4_____ around the

Sun. All of the planets are trapped by the

_____5_____ of the Sun.

The Solar System is big. But all of the

_____6_____ we can see are far outside the

Solar System.

Planet data 1 – other worlds

The Solar System is made up of planets and their moons in orbit around the Sun. We'd find that the planets would all be very different places if we could visit them.

The sky at night is very, very beautiful. People have looked at it and wondered about it for thousands of years. They spotted that some of the small points of light in the sky do not seem to move in a simple way. There were only a few of these and they were given their own name – the **planets**.

In the past, most people guessed that the Earth was the centre of everything. They guessed that the Sun and the planets and the stars all went around the Earth. But that couldn't explain the way that the planets seemed to move in more complicated ways across the sky. Then a Polish monk called Copernicus explained that there was another, simpler way of understanding the planets, the Earth and the Sun. He said that the Earth could actually *be* a planet itself, and that the Earth and the *other* planets were all going around the Sun. Copernicus wrote about the **revolutions** of the Earth and planets.

This meant that the Earth was not the centre of everything. To the people of Copernicus' day this was an amazingly new idea. Most people didn't like such a new idea. So, even now when someone suggests something so incredibly new, we say that their idea is *revolutionary*.

Figure 1 Revolutions of the planets around the Sun. Nobody has ever seen the sight shown on this page. We can only imagine what the Solar System would be like if we could go outside it and look back. It wouldn't look quite like the picture here because we have exaggerated the sizes of the planets. From outside the Solar System the Earth would be too small to see at all. This picture also shows a comet. A comet is much smaller than a planet. It moves around the Sun, but sometimes it is very near to the Sun and sometimes it is very far away.

Planet data

Average distances from the Sun, in millions of kilometres.

Mercury	58
Venus	108
Earth	150
Mars	228
Jupiter	778
Saturn	1430
Uranus	2870
Neptune	4500
Pluto	5900

Force of gravity on a bag of sugar on the planet's surface, in newtons

Mercury	4
Venus	9
Earth	10
Mars	4
Jupiter	26
Saturn	10
Uranus	8
Neptune	12
Pluto	1

Number of moons

Mercury	0
Venus	0
Earth	1
Mars	2
Jupiter	16
Saturn	>30
Uranus	15
Neptune	8
Pluto	1

Surface temperature in °C

Mercury	−170 to 400
Venus	350 to 475
Earth	−80 to 50
Mars	−125 to 20
Jupiter	−150
Saturn	−200 to −150
Uranus	−220
Neptune	−220
Pluto	−250

Questions

1 Which of the planets is most like Earth in

   a) its distance from the Sun?

   b) the number of moons it has?

   c) how heavy a bag of sugar (or anything else) is on its surface?

2 a) Make charts or graphs of the information in the tables on this page.

   b) Draw labelled pictures of the planets. Think about the sizes of the planets in relation to each other.

   c) Combine all of these together into a poster to go on the wall.

   Use a computer to help you with this work.

3 Choose the planet you would most like to visit. Write a paragraph about what you might see if you were on the surface of that planet.

Remember

Match the words to the spaces.

**Pluto   Pluto   smaller   Moon   moons
Venus   planets   Sun   forces   Mercury**

The Solar System contains ____1____ travelling round the Sun. Most of the planets have ____2____. Moons are ____3____ objects that travel close to their planets. The Earth has only one moon, called the ____4____.

The planets are at different distances from the ____5____. ____6____ is the closest and ____7____ is the furthest away. ____8____ is the hottest and ____9____ is the coldest. The planets have different sizes. There are different ____10____ of gravity on their surfaces.

Planet data II – seasons on the planets

Different planets have different patterns of days, years and seasons.

The planets are all at different distances from the Sun. So they must make different journeys around the Sun. Mercury is the closest to the Sun. It takes the shortest time to go round once. Pluto is the furthest from the Sun and it takes the longest.

As the planets speed through space they also spin, like crazy fairground rides. We spend our whole lives on one of these fairground rides. We speed round the Sun, once in every Earth year. At the same time we spin. It takes just one Earth day to make a complete spin. As we spin, we sometimes face towards the Sun. We have a name for times like that – it's called daytime. It is the spin of the Earth that carries us into light and darkness every day.

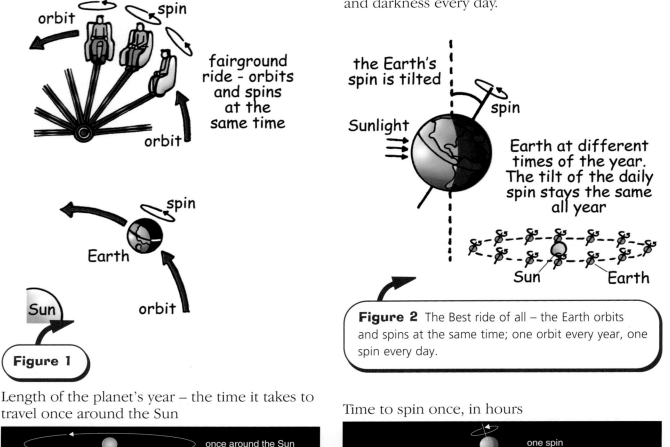

fairground ride - orbits and spins at the same time

Figure 1

the Earth's spin is tilted

Sunlight

Earth at different times of the year. The tilt of the daily spin stays the same all year

Figure 2 The Best ride of all – the Earth orbits and spins at the same time; one orbit every year, one spin every day.

Length of the planet's year – the time it takes to travel once around the Sun

		once around the Sun
Mercury	88 Earth days	= 1 Mercury year
Venus	225 Earth days	= 1 Venus year
Earth	365.25 Earth days	= 1 Earth year
Mars	687 Earth days	= 1 Mars year
Jupiter	12 Earth years	= 1 Jupiter year
Saturn	30 Earth years	= 1 Saturn year
Uranus	84 Earth years	= 1 Uranus year
Neptune	165 Earth years	= 1 Neptune year
Pluto	248 Earth years	= 1 Pluto year

Time to spin once, in hours

		one spin
Mercury	1416	= 1 Mercury day
Venus	5832	= 1 Venus day
Earth	24	= 1 Earth day
Mars	25	= 1 Mars day
Jupiter	10	= 1 Jupiter day
Saturn	10	= 1 Saturn day
Uranus	11	= 1 Uranus day
Neptune	16	= 1 Neptune day
Pluto	6	= 1 Pluto day

The tilt in the Earth's spin means that for part of each year, the northern half is tilted towards the Sun. The northern half is called the northern **hemisphere**. At this time the Sun shines more from overhead and the weather is warmer. It's called summer. At the same time the southern half is tilted away from the Sun. There the sunshine is not so strong and it is winter. Six months later the Earth has moved halfway round the Sun. Then it's the southern hemisphere that gets the Sun more overhead, and it's the turn of the northern half to have winter.

In the winter the Sun does not rise so high in the sky, because we are tilted away from the Sun. Also we do not spend so much of each day in the light of the Sun. It goes dark in the afternoon, and gets light again quite late in the morning.

Tilt of spin

Mercury	7°
Venus	3°
Earth	24°
Mars	26°
Jupiter	3°
Saturn	27°
Uranus	88°
Neptune	29°
Pluto	50°

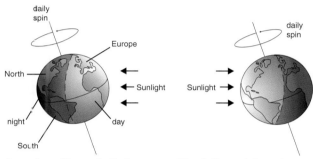

daily spin

Europe

North

Sunlight

Sunlight

night

day

South

At some times of the year the Southern half of the Earth is tilted towards the Sun. In the north we have winter and we spend more of each day in darkness.

When it's Summer in the north we are tilted towards the Sun. We don't spend so long in darkness.

Figure 3 It is the tilt of the Earth that gives us the seasons.

Questions

1 Which planet is most like the Earth in
   a) the time taken to go around the Sun?
   b) the time taken to spin once?
   c) tilt of its spin?

2 a) How many times have you been around the Sun?
   b) If you'd lived all your life on Jupiter, how many times would you have gone around the Sun? What is your age in Jupiter years?

3 On Venus there isn't much difference between summer and winter. Can you explain why?

4 How long is a Neptune year? How long is a Neptune day? On Neptune how could you tell the difference between the summer and the winter?

Remember

Match the words to the spaces.

winter	spin	Earth	year	northern
away	tilted	seasons	hemisphere	

The time that the Earth takes to go around the Sun is called one _____**1**_____.

The length of time that the Earth takes to make one _____**2**_____ is called one Earth day.

The spin of the Earth is _____**3**_____. The tilt stays the same all year. Sometimes the _____**4**_____ half of the Earth is tilted towards the Sun, and sometimes the southern half is tilted towards the Sun. That is why we have _____**5**_____.

In _____**6**_____ we spend longer in darkness, because then it is our _____**7**_____ of the planet that is tilted _____**8**_____ from the Sun.

Closer

Activity

Space missions

1   These are the names of some space missions to other planets.

- Pioneer 11
- Voyager 1
- Voyager 2
- Mars Express
- Mars Rover
- Cassini-Huygens
- Cassini
- Huygens
- Venus Express

Find out more about one of them. You could do an internet search, using one of the names as your search word. Make a poster, a leaflet or a PowerPoint presentation about the mission. Who organised the mission? What did they want to find out?

2   By sending spacecraft and astronauts to other planets, and some of their moons, we find out more about the universe we live in. For example, we can study weather systems on other planets and compare them with weather systems on Earth. This can help us to understand our own planet better. But space missions are expensive.

Governments must use taxpayers' money to send rockets into space. Should we forget about planets and spend the money on other things?

3   Write a story about an imaginary journey through the Solar System. Your journey could be to just one planet or to several. These are some of the things you could include in your story:

- How far will you have to travel?
- What will the Sun look like from different places?
- Will you have to go to sleep during daylight?
- How long might you have to wait for it to get light?
- How heavy will your body feel? What about other objects?
- What protection will your body need?
- Will the sky look the same as it does from Earth?
- Do you think you will find other living things?

4   Have a look back at the chapter opener. Have you become more confident or changed any of your ideas about The Solar System?

Confused words

Don't be caught out when these words are used. They have a special meaning in science.

Word	Common English meaning	Science meaning
Absorb	He used a cloth to absorb the water he'd spilt.	Most substances absorb light.
Acid	She has a very acid tongue.	Acids are corrosive substances that taste sour.
Antenna	Can you wiggle the antenna to pick up a better TV picture?	A structure found on the head of animals, usually to detect sound or smell.
Atmosphere	They didn't stay at the restaurant because it had no atmosphere.	Atmosphere is the layer of gas around a planet.
Boiling	Its boiling hot!	The boiling point of water is 100°C – it's never that hot.
Cell	He was locked away in a cell for five years.	A cell is an electrical energy store. A group of cells make a battery. OR The basic unit of which plants and animals are made up.
Concentration	Homework needs concentration.	Concentrated solutions have a lot of solid dissolved in them.
Condensing	I am condensing my argument into one sentence.	When a vapour turns into a liquid on a cold surface, it is condensing.
Conductor	The conductor was in charge of the orchestra.	An electrical conductor lets electric current flow through it and a thermal conductor lets energy flow through it.
Current	The current situation is difficult.	Current is an electrical flow.
Dense / density	He's really dense.	Density is heaviness for its size.
Drag	She had to drag the truth out of him.	Drag is a force that resists motion.
Elastic	You use elastic in clothes.	Elastic means a substance stretches but goes back to its original shape.
Element	I think the element in the kettle has burned out.	A substance that contains only one type of atom.
Energy	That boy has got too much energy!	Heating and cooling involve transfer of energy. When a force acts and something moves, that also involves transfer of energy.
Evaporate	She could feel her enthusiasm evaporate.	Particles of a liquid escape into the surroundings when it evaporates.
Force(s)	The police force.	A force is a push or a pull.

Confused words

Word	Common English meaning	Science meaning
Freezing	It's freezing cold.	The freezing point of water is 0°C – it can be that cold when it's frosty.
Gas	Light the gas (for a cooker).	A gas can be many substances e.g. oxygen.
Habitat	Shall we go to Habitat and buy some furniture?	The home for a group of organisms.
Hip	That's quite a hip outfit you're wearing!	A part of the skeleton that supports the legs.
Host	Will you be the host of the party on Saturday night?	The animal that a parasite lives inside.
Humerus	That comedian thinks she's humerous (note the different spelling).	The bone that connects the shoulder and elbow.
Impulse	I feel a little impulsive today, I might have an impulse buy in the shops!	The electric charge that travels along a nerve fibre.
Indicator	Indicators are orange winking lights on cars.	An indicator is a material that changes colour in solutions of different acidity.
Ions	Iron is a metal that can go rusty.	Ion sounds similar to iron, but it is a particle in a chemical change.
Irritant	That boy is an irritant!	An irritant is a chemical that affects the skin – it is a hazard.
Kingdom	As your sovereign I rule this kingdom!	All living things are divided into five kingdoms.
Lift	They took the lift to the fourth floor.	Lift is an upwards force on the wings of a bird or a plane.
Lime water	Lime is a green fruit like a lemon, and a white chalky powder.	Lime water is made with chalky powder not with fruit.
Liquid	I need a drink of liquid.	Liquids can be many different substances – not just water based.
Mass	She goes to Mass every Sunday.	Mass is a measure of the amount of material an object has.
Material	What colour material do you want for your new dress?	All the stuff things are made from.
Matter	What's the matter?	Matter is the stuff we are made from.
Moment	Wait just a moment!	A moment is a turning effect of a force.
Negative	He felt very negative about going to school this morning.	A battery has a negative terminal.
Neutralise	A large police force will neutralise the threat of disorder.	Acids will neutralise alkalis in a chemical change.
Normal	Everything is normal here.	A normal is a line which is at 90° to a surface.
Organ	On Sundays I play the organ in church.	A group of tissues working together.

Word	Common English meaning	Science meaning
Peat	Hi Pete, where are you going? (Note the spelling.)	Rotted vegetable matter formed thousands of years ago.
Pest	You are a pest during the summer holidays!	An animal, often an insect, that is a nuisance.
Plastic	A plastic washing up bowl.	Plastic means a substance stretches and stays in the new shape, like putty.
Positive	The results of the test were positive.	A battery has a positive terminal.
Power	We have the power to arrest you.	Power is a measure of how quickly energy is transferred, such as by a kettle or a lamp.
Pressure	I feel under pressure to pass exams.	Pressure is the force per unit of area.
Pure	Not harmful.	Contains only one substance.
Range	The eggs are free range.	A range of values is the difference between the highest and the lowest.
Ray	You are my little ray of sunshine.	A ray is a very thin line that we draw to show a pathway of light.
Reflect	Reflect on your behaviour.	Surfaces can reflect light.
Renewable	His membership of the sports club is renewable every year.	A renewable energy resource is one that will not run out.
Salt(s)	Salt and vinegar on chips.	Table salt is one kind of salt made in neutralisation reactions.
Saturated	I got caught in the rain and I'm saturated!	A saturated solution will not dissolve any more solute.
Scale	Fish have scales on their skin.	Measuring instruments have scales with marks and numbers.
School	Off you go to school today, no arguments please!	A group of animals that live in water, e.g. a school of dolphins.
Solution	Have you found the solution to the puzzle?	A solution is made by dissolving a solute in a solvent.
Thrust	She thrust her face into other people's business.	Thrust is a driving force.
Transfer	Blogtown United have put their goalkeeper on the transfer list.	Energy can transfer from place to place and from system to system.
Unbalanced	If I have to put up with much more of this my mind will become unbalanced.	Unbalanced force produces acceleration.
Unit	They've chosen some nice new kitchen units.	Degrees Celsius, newtons, metres and seconds are all examples of units of measurement.
Vacuum	He decided to vacuum the floor.	A vacuum is a space with no air or other material.
Variable	The weather was variable when I went on holiday.	A variable is a quantity that can change.
Work	I did eight hours hard work today.	Work is a kind of energy transfer that happens when force changes the motion of an object.

Glossary

Glossary

Glossary